A YOUNG CATHOLIC'S GUIDE TO
SPIRITUAL WARFARE

Fr. William Peckman

MATER
MEDIA

Nihil obstat
Reverend Dylan Schrader, Ph.D.
Censor Liborum
December 2, 2021

Imprimatur
The Most Reverend W. Shawn McKnight, S.T.D
Bishop of Jefferson City
December 9, 2021

The *Nihil obstat* and *Imprimatur* are declarations that the material is free from doctrinal or moral error, and thus is granted permission to publish in accord with c. 827 of the Code of Canon Law. No implication is contained herein that those who have granted the *Nihil obstat* and *Imprimatur* agree with the content, opinions, or statements expressed.

Copyright William Peckman © 2021. All rights reserved.

No part of this book may be used or reproduced by any means, graphic, electronic, or mechanical, including photocopying, recording, taping or by any information storage retrieval system without the written permission of the publisher.

Published by Mater Media
St. Louis, Missouri
www.matermedia.org

Editor: Kari Sherman
Initial Edit: Jeff Leslie
Design: Trese Gloriod

Printed in the USA.

978-1-7365190-6-6

TABLE OF CONTENTS

INTRODUCTION 1

CHAPTER 1: WHY ENGAGE? 4

CHAPTER 2: THE DEVIL, HIS TOOLS, YOUR WEAPONS 8

CHAPTER 3: THE CORE BATTLE PLAN 16

CHAPTER 4: PRIDE 20

CHAPTER 5: LUST 30

CHAPTER 6: GREED 42

CHAPTER 7: ENVY 52

CHAPTER 8: GLUTTONY 62

CHAPTER 9: WRATH 72

CHAPTER 10: SLOTH 82

CHAPTER 11: BEING A HEROIC WARRIOR 92

APPENDIX OF PRAYERS 96

INTRODUCTION

As a young Catholic, you may have heard a version of this 19th Century quote: "The greatest trick the devil ever pulled was to convince the world he doesn't exist." If you look at society today, it appears like his ploy is in full swing. In homilies and seminaries, the devil, the demonic, and Hell are rarely discussed - How are we supposed to combat something we aren't taught is there?

Although church leadership tends to ignore them, and the Western World categorizes them as fodder for horror movies, the *Catechism of the Catholic Church* and exorcists certainly teach about their existence. Fr. Gabriele Amorth, the Chief Exorcist of Rome stated in a Vanity Fair article from 2016 that, "Today Satan rules the world...And yes, Satan is in the Vatican."

So, how did we get to this point? There are a variety of reasons, but the devil has used two worldviews to help his efforts: secularism and universalism. Secularism says that anything that can't be measured scientifically, likely does not exist. It shows up around us as the dismissal of anything supernatural, either because it's "too hard to believe" or we don't "need" it.

Many of you are too young to have heard John Lennon's famous song "Imagine," but in it he sings of a reality without Heaven, Hell, or religion. He paints a lyrical picture that all mankind needs to do is come together to stamp out injustice, hate, and want, all on our own. Look around. How is that working out for us?

Besides the complete dismissal of God in secularism, we have universalism sweeping the globe. Universalism says that if there is a higher power, all people will eventually end up in heaven. It denies that Jesus is the only way to the Father and allows man to be his own god without worrying about the consequences. What a great relief to believe that our sin will go unpunished when we die – comforting, but not reality. Both world views are lies, and both have contributed to evil running rampant.

As young Catholics, you know the truth is what the Church has proclaimed from the very beginning. But just knowing the truth is not enough. That's where this book comes in.

The devil doesn't show up in your life with horns and a pitchfork, he comes disguised as everything you've ever wanted. He deceives us with what he knows – rebellion, and he turns the world into an endless array of temptations and entices us with lies. The good news is that the choice is yours. You don't have to follow the dangling carrot; you can choose good over evil. Whether you've been taught it before or not, the devil and his minions are there. This book will teach you how to use the tools God has given you to fight back. You can choose to be on God's side, which is the side that will lead you not to worldly pleasures, but to the greatest pleasure of all - everlasting life.

As a disclaimer, I write this book as one who hasn't always fought well. I have been savaged on the battlefield and still struggle to conquer temptation every day. There was a time in my life where I too followed the enticing calls of popular worldviews. As a professed agnostic I was quite happy to be my own god. I wasn't a horrible person and didn't engage in illegal behavior. In fact, I was a fairly stand-up kind of guy; however, being my own god allowed me to justify my favored sins. I let anger settle in my soul that caused me to lash out when tired or irritated. It enabled me to rationalize lust as 'adult choices,' leading to porn, pre-marital sex, and self-abuse. It granted me free reign of greed, to make my life about the pursuit of power, wealth, and pleasure. I was following all the shiny things, not realizing the shimmer was from those hidden horns. Thanks be to God, He saved me from the destruction I was immersed in, and He can save you too.

In Sun Tzu's classic, *The Art of War,* he says "If you know the enemy and you know yourself, you need not fear the result of a hundred battles. If you know yourself but not the enemy, for every victory gained you will also suffer a defeat. If you know neither the enemy nor yourself, you will succumb in every battle." This handbook is about knowing your enemy and yourself, but also knowing the God that will bring you to victory. You will learn how the enemy shows up in the deadly sins, which lead to all the others. You will get to know yourself better by reflecting on how those sins are affecting your life. I will introduce the battle plans that God has given us to fight the enemy, the same ones I've used in my three decades of priesthood. You will discover how to cultivate virtues, utilize worship and the sacraments, and create targeted mortifications.

WITH GOD ON YOUR SIDE, YOU NEED NOT FEAR THE RESULT OF YOUR BATTLES.

But make no mistake, the battle wages whether we are engaged or not. The devil will take as much as he can get until he completely disfigures your soul. You are either laying on the ground defenseless, or you can choose to take up arms, and like St. Peter slipping under the waves say, "Lord, save me!"

CHAPTER 1:
WHY ENGAGE?

Before we get to know our enemy (to prepare us for battle), we need to talk about why to engage in the first place. Why fight the devil and temptation? Why not just give in? You're only human after all.

There are plenty of reasons why the fight is worth it. The obvious one is that your soul, and where you will spend eternity, is on the line; however, the decision to engage also greatly impacts your life on Earth. Your decisions have consequences, good and bad, that sometimes last a lifetime. When you take up arms you become a better follower of Christ, lead a more fulfilling life, and encourage others to do the same. As you win battles, you become a better person – a better child, parent, sibling, friend, spouse, etc.

This confrontation with evil is also not just about you. Whether you have found your vocation or not, you are fighting for others. As a priest, God has placed a portion of His flock (my parishes) in my care. I battle for them. If you are married, God has blessed you with a spouse, and maybe children, whom you go to war for. If you are single, you may be brawling for your siblings, your friends, or your future family. Sometimes it's *hard* to do the right thing, but in those times, it is love of the people you fight for that will push you forward.

Love is the driving force for all of this. It keeps us going. When someone loves, they don't hesitate to place themselves in harm's way to protect what is irreplaceable. I have seen many images of soldiers in battle who carry pictures of their loved ones, to serve as a reminder about who they are risking it all for. Love motivates us to be heroic. It beats down the fear.

Although love for the ones we care about can motivate our efforts in spiritual warfare, 'agape' is essential for long-term success. Agape is a Greek word that references the highest form of love. It is the kind of

JESUS SHOWS US HOW MUCH HE TRULY LOVES US AND WANTS TO PROTECT US.

sacrificial love that God is, gives to us, and commands us to show our neighbor. When it comes to this type of love and laying it all on the line, Jesus is the perfect example for us to look to.

Jesus calls Himself "the Good Shepherd." In biblical times, shepherding was a dangerous profession. Many times, the shepherd would have to protect their flock from robbers and predators by getting in between the sheep and the danger. Jesus had such an agape love for us that He laid down His life sacrificially. It is that love that we suffer greatly without, and that is needed for this battle.

So, where do we learn how to cultivate this type of love in our own lives? I would suggest we start at the foot of the Cross. Here, Jesus shows us how much He truly loves us and wants to protect us. We can see His love for the Father when he says, "not my will, but yours be done." Agape love, when cultivated, will lead us to this same conclusion. We'll begin to see that God loves us as He loves his Son, and that He will give us the victory over the devil, just like He gave that victory to Jesus.

I also suggest spending time in Eucharistic Adoration. There we come into Jesus's very presence as He pours Himself out in the Eucharist for love of us. There are times where I pray before the Blessed Sacrament and can do little more than repeatedly say, "Lord Jesus, teach me to love the Father as you love Him, and to see that the Father loves me as much as He loves you!"

Agape love spurs me on to engage in whatever temptation comes that day for the sake of those Jesus has placed under my care. I want to sacrifice for them as Jesus has done for me. It motivates us to *want* to change and grow in our relationship with God. We desire to join the angelic forces and learn to use the weapons we've been given. It gives us the strength to get back up after we've been beaten down.

We can also turn to Our Blessed Mother to learn what love looks like. She knows, more so than anyone, what it means to fully love Jesus and to be completely loved by Him. Her love took her through many sorrows, all the way to the foot of the Cross. Many statues of Mary show her foot crushing a snake. Her rosary is a powerful tool in our fight against the devil. Reciting it is not magical incantation, it is powerful intercession from the one who crushes Satan's head.

Finally young Catholics, as we start this journey, do not be afraid! We battle with the love of Jesus and the aid of Our Blessed Mother and the saints, along with St. Michael and the heavenly hosts. We have a mighty team!

Speaking of team, now is as good a place as any to remind you to surround yourself with like-minded warriors who will support you. I have seen many pictures over the years of injured soldiers being carried by their battalion mates. Sometimes we are the injured one in need of assistance, and other times we are needed to rally around our brothers and sisters in Christ. You and I are comrades against a fierce enemy who can, and will, be defeated. When we choose to engage in this battle and cultivate agape love, we follow our Lord Jesus into the breach.

CHAPTER 2:
THE DEVIL, HIS TOOLS, YOUR WEAPONS

As we established in the introduction, the enemy exists, and we put ourselves in monumental danger when we pretend he doesn't. Removing the supernatural elements from our Catholic faith is like taking peanut butter out of a PBJ - it completely transforms it into something else. If we see the Church as a mere man-made institution on a human mission, we don't just miss the bullseye, we've aimed our arrow in the completely opposite direction.

When we acknowledge the enemy's existence, the spiritual battlefield becomes visible to us; God on one side and the devil on the other. Can you imagine fighting in a war you don't even know you're engaged in? You'd have no chance! You're essentially a sitting duck for the enemy and don't even know you're quacking. If you prefer not to be the devil's dinner, keep reading.

Before we look at how the enemy works, we need to understand what's at stake here. In traditional war, your life is on the line, and possibly the freedom of your country. In spiritual warfare, you are fighting for your soul, which is far more precious. If victorious, you get to place your flag in Heaven next to all the saints' who have come before you and claim your prize of eternal life with your Creator. What a glorious trophy! One worth laying it all on the line for.

God created us to be in eternal relationship with Him. He wants us in Heaven for all eternity, but we don't get an all-access pass with a "Get out of Hell free" card. In Matthew 25: 34 Jesus describes the Last Judgment, "Then the king will say to those on his right, 'Come, you who are blessed by my Father. Inherit the kingdom prepared for you from the foundation of the world.'" This all sounds great, and then we get to verse 41. "Then he will say to those on his left, 'Depart from me, you accursed, into the eternal fire prepared for the devil and his angels.'" This shows us that although humans were created for Heaven, we can (and do) reject that invitation.

So now that we've established that our enemy exists, that we're on a spiritual battlefield, and that our souls are at stake, let's take a look at *who* we are up against.

THE DEVIL

Our adversary goes by many names, but his game is always the same – to get us to follow in his footsteps and reject our relationship with God. Let's see what we can learn about his schemes by examining a few of them.

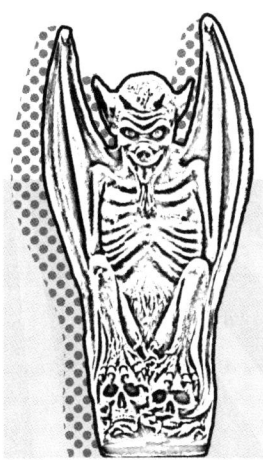

Lucifer = means "light bearer" (An archangel who had fallen because of his contempt for God's plan. He was so stirred by anger over the creation of humanity that he resolved to turn God's creation on Him.) ***Take away:*** *The devil can appear as something good and desirable. He uses deception to trick us.*

Satan = means 'the accuser' (In the book of Job we see him accuse Job of being faithful only because God blessed him with wealth and health.) ***Take away:*** *Satan may accuse us of things too. These accusations may be true or false, but he ultimately uses them to manipulate us.*

Father of Lies = the supreme liar (He told the first lie in recorded history in the Garden of Eden. He spins a web of deceit.) ***Take away:*** *The devil's language is lies. They all circle around the one he himself bought - that you can have an eternally fulfilling identity outside of God.*

As you can see by his various monikers, he is a lying, deceptive accuser. On the surface he's not very attractive, but he is an expert at disguise. Luckily, he can't make you do anything. He doesn't have the ability to override your free will and force you into sin, so he uses his primary weapon — temptation. Let's peek at his playbook, by examining how he used this tool against Eve.

HIS TOOLS

God gives us some important information about our adversary in Genesis 3:1-8. Here we learn how the devil uses questions, packages temptations, twists truths, and spits lies.

In verse one, Satan says to Eve, "Did God really say, 'You shall not eat from any of the trees in the garden?'" Notice how he addresses her with a question they both already know the answer to. He doesn't ask it to get a response, he does so to plant a seed of division in Eve's heart, inferring that God does not want what is good for her. At this point she still trusts in God's providence and refutes this first lie in verses two and three. "The woman said to the serpent, 'From the fruit of the trees of the garden we may eat; but from the fruit of the tree which is in the middle of the garden, God has said 'You shall not eat from it or touch it, or you will die.'"

The devil continues undeterred, revealing his relentlessness. In the next two verses, he follows up the first lie with an even more powerful one. "The serpent said to the woman, 'You certainly will not die! For God knows that on the day you eat from it your eyes will be opened, and you will become like

ENTERS IN

God, knowing good and evil.'" This temptation is the prototype of each one since. In essence, he's encouraging her to deny God's lordship and rebel against Him, the same thing he tempts us to do today.

He knew that if Adam and Eve ate the fruit, they would know evil (they already knew the good), but he also knew that they could not actually become like God. Remember, he is the 'Father of Lies,' and his goal is always to destroy our relationship with God, which he does by getting us to fall into sin.

It's important to note that the devil tempted Eve with a fruit that was pleasing to her senses, he didn't use strained beets. He presents an evil as something good and desirable, without explaining the consequences. If he showed us the misery that would *actually* follow from caving to temptation, we would be slow, if not impervious, to it. But in verse six, Eve sees that "the tree was good for food, and that it was a delight to the eyes" and eats the fruit. She is misled and falls.

This simple act of rebellion left us all with the stain of original sin. Baptism erases this when we are given sanctifying grace; however, we still have to deal with the repercussions of the Pandora's Box Adam and Eve opened. The *Catechism* tells us that because of this event, "human nature is weakened in its powers; subject to ignorance, suffering, and the dominion of death; and inclined to sin" (CCC 418). We are also told that the consequences of original sin summon us to spiritual battle (see CCC 405).

Because of the events that transpired in Genesis, we are now inclined to sin. Since we know sin damages or severs our relationship with God, we should avoid it at all costs. To help us do so, let's establish what sin is.

Sin is like the hammer in the devil's toolbox because it smashes our relationship with God. You can check out paragraphs 1849 and 1850 in the *Catechism of the Catholic Church* for definitions of sin, but there are two types we must be aware of: mortal sin and venial sin.

Mortal sin is a grave violation of God's law and turns us away from Him (CCC 1855). To be a grave matter, it must violate the Ten Commandments, and you must have committed them with *full knowledge* and *deliberate consent* (CCC 1857 & 1858).

Once we commit a mortal sin, we fall into a *state* of mortal sin. This means we have severed our relationship with God. If we die in this state unrepentant, we are where the devil wants us - out of relationship with God and on his eternal team of darkness.

After our baptisms, the damage caused by mortal sin requires the Sacrament of Reconciliation to restore the sanctifying grace lost by our choices. Therefore, it is essential to go to Confession as soon as possible after a mortal sin has been committed.

If one or more of the criteria mentioned above is missing, or the sin isn't a violation of the Ten Commandments, it is known as a venial sin. Sometimes we act out of panic or fear and diminish the use of free will. Other times we lack the understanding that what we do is sinful through unintentional ignorance. That does not mean venial sins aren't sinful or don't need forgiveness. These sins damage, but don't sever the relationship with God. If left unattended, they form the habit of sin, which makes mortal sin easier to do (see CCC 1862-1863).

The repair for venial sin is covered within the Mass during the Penitential Rite. Near the beginning of Mass, we are asked by the priest to call to mind our sins, then comes the Kyrie (Lord have Mercy) or the Confiteor (I confess to Almighty God), and an absolution is given: "May Almighty God have mercy on us, forgive us our sins, and lead us to everlasting life." An Act of Contrition can be done in private.

Avoiding both types of sin assists you greatly in battle. The premise of this battle is simple — Will you choose to be God's child or His rival? You can't be both. You are fighting for your soul. Because of our innate desire to sin (concupiscence), our natural defenses are not enough. The devil knows the terrain well and will exploit our weaknesses. He will use your unstable areas against you and then wedge them between you and God – eventually it is no longer the devil you are fighting, but your Creator.

God is well aware of our weakened state and because he cares for us, He gives us armor and weapons to fight with. He provides these out of His love, and His undeserved help, known as grace. Let's look at some of these defenses.

YOUR WEAPONS

In Ephesians 6:10-18, St. Paul tells us, "Finally, be strong in the Lord and in the strength of His might. Put on the full armor of God, so that you will be able to stand firm against the schemes of the devil. For our struggle is not against flesh and blood, but against the rulers, against the powers, against the world forces of this darkness, against the

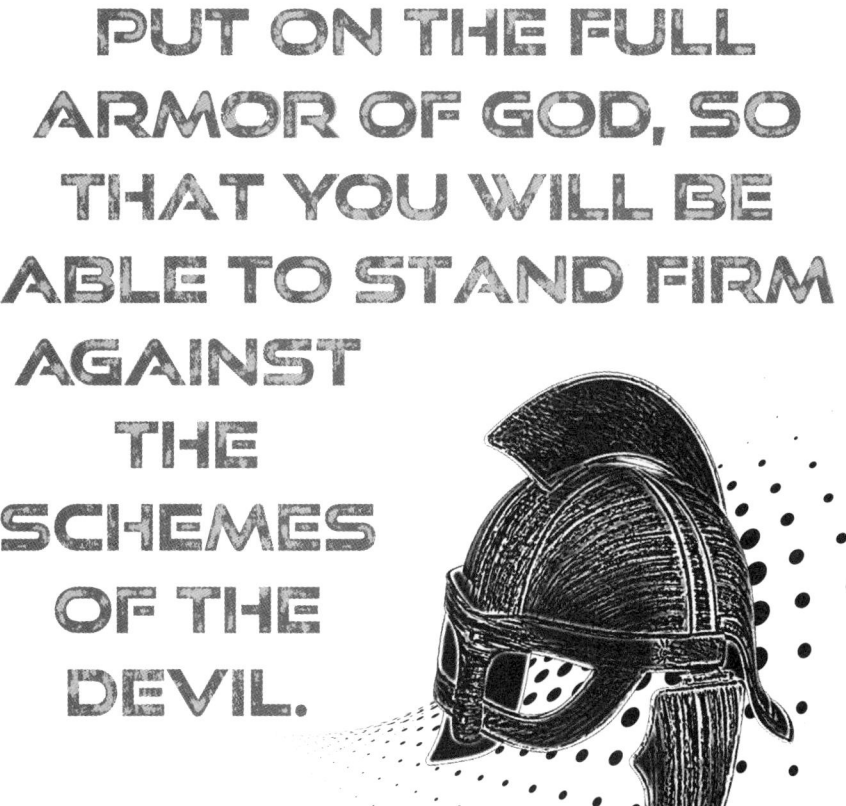

PUT ON THE FULL ARMOR OF GOD, SO THAT YOU WILL BE ABLE TO STAND FIRM AGAINST THE SCHEMES OF THE DEVIL.

spiritual forces of wickedness in the heavenly places. Therefore, take up the full armor of God, so that you will be able to resist on the evil day, and having done everything, to stand firm. Stand firm therefore, having belted your waist with truth, and having put on the breastplate of righteousness, and having strapped on your feet the preparation of the gospel of peace; in addition to all, taking up the shield of faith with which you will be able to extinguish all the flaming arrows of the evil one. And take the helmet of salvation and the sword of the Spirit, which is the word of God. With every prayer and request, pray at all times in the Spirit, and with this in view, be alert with all perseverance and every request for all the saints."

Thankfully, God doesn't expect you to fight this ongoing battle alone. The world would like you to believe that fighting and beating the devil is just a matter of picking up the right self-help book. The world is wrong. You need God's grace. Why? Because you cannot fight a spiritual battle against a powerful spiritual enemy with mere human wisdom or effort. Luckily, you have the spiritual aids mentioned by St. Paul...but wait, there's more!

As Catholics, you have the sacramental life of the Church. Each of the seven sacraments spurs you on to do battle in the way God has called you to (this will look different for everyone).

You also have the Church Militant and the Church Triumphant on your side. The Church Militant consists of 1.5 billion members who are on Earth right now, supporting you in prayer and aiding you in battle. Unfortunately, that Church can be divided and wracked by sin herself. The devil likes it when we fight each other instead of him. Don't be part of the problem!

The Church Triumphant consists of the saints and angels who assist us in our battle with their prayers and protection. The saints have conquered the devil. They know how to do it, so follow in their footsteps. The angels stand as our God-given protectors in the fight. We can find great consolation knowing we never enter the battlefield alone.

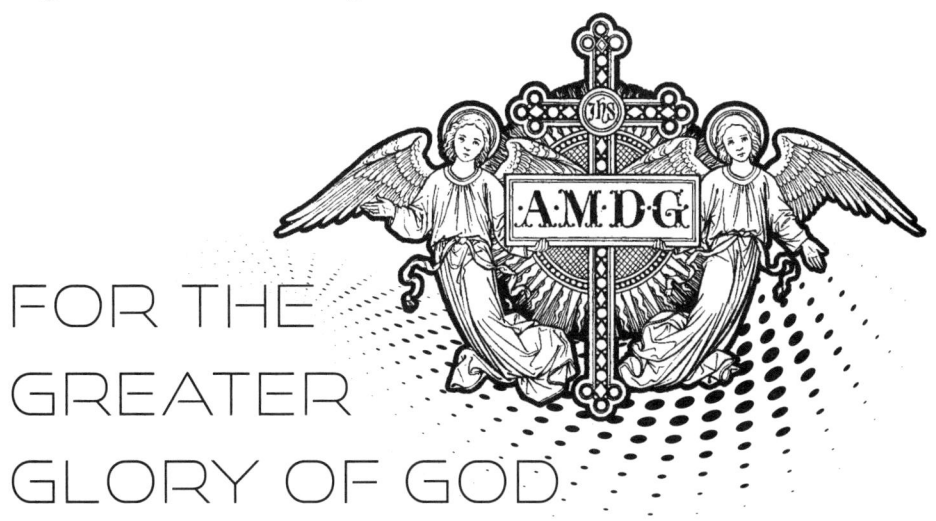

FOR THE GREATER GLORY OF GOD.

CHAPTER 3:
THE CORE BATTLE PLAN

We've established that we have access to the armor and weapons we need for this battle, but knowledge without action is useless. We can't just sit back idly; we must draw up a battle plan.

Each of the following chapters will focus on the key pressure points the devil likes to hit - the seven deadly sins: pride, sloth, wrath, greed, gluttony, envy, and lust. Each of them is the result of a big lie and has specific actions to

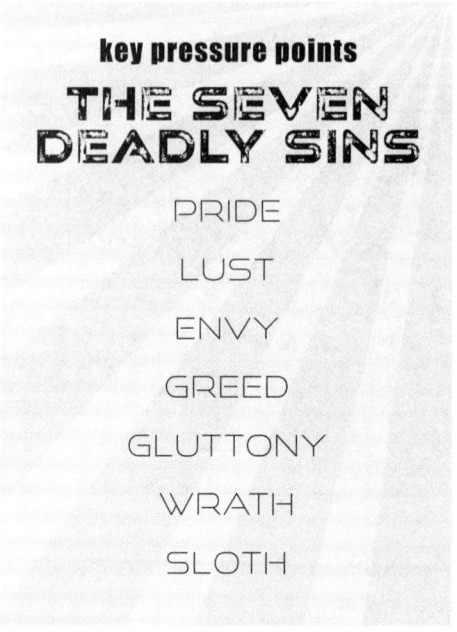

key pressure points

THE SEVEN DEADLY SINS

PRIDE

LUST

ENVY

GREED

GLUTTONY

WRATH

SLOTH

help you conquer it (those will be discussed at the end of their respective chapters); however, there are eight core measures that are essential to spiritual warfare and will help conquer every capital sin. We will dive deeper into these throughout the book, but here is a summary that you can easily refer to:

IDENTIFY WHERE YOUR DEFENSES ARE WEAK:

The devil is good at identifying where your walls have been breached, and he attacks where you are weak. You need to figure out where your defenses are crumbling or non-existent because when you *know* your weaknesses, you give yourself an edge. You are unique, and your defenses might be lowered in a place where someone else has a wall of steel. Reflect as you read and figure out where you need reinforcements and then focus your efforts there. Examine your conscience often.

PRAY:

Prayer teaches us dependence on God and helps us engage in battle. It is also our main way to communicate with God, and communication is key in every relationship. Learn to *listen* for God's voice instead of just doing all the talking. There are also many great spiritual warfare prayers, some are included at the back of this book.

MAKE USE OF CONFESSION:

Think of the Sacrament of Reconciliation as the field hospital where you can seek healing from the wounds inflicted on your soul by sin. Exorcists have said that it is more powerful than an exorcism in chasing the devil away. In Confession you are identifying where you have allowed the devil to get into your life via sin and wiping the slate clean. The devil may try to use the same access point repeatedly, but the sacramental grace given here helps you solidify those weak areas over time. Confession puts you in a state of grace which enables you to receive the Eucharist.

CLING TO THE EUCHARIST:

The Eucharist is Jesus in Body, Blood, Soul, and Divinity. It will give you the strength you need to maneuver on the battlefield. It is powerful against the devil, from both a defensive and offensive position. I also highly recommend Eucharistic Adoration. Having face-to-face times of prayer with Jesus, especially if you feel weak, is important and necessary.

WE CAN'T JUST SIT BACK IDLY;

EMPLOY THE LONG-STANDING WEAPONS OF ABSTINENCE AND FASTING:

Fasting and abstinence help us detach from worldliness and rein in our appetites (the devil counts on us being a slave to those). In the gospels of Matthew and Mark, Jesus says that some demons "can only be driven out by prayer and fasting" (Matthew 17:21, Mark 9:29). The devil does not like to lose ground that he has gained, so sins that have become habitual (especially sins of the flesh), are long, hard-fought battles. It's important to use all the weapons we can.

DEVELOP A DEVOTIONAL LIFE:

Pretty much every devotion we have in the Church is a useful tool in directly combating the devil. I particularly encourage praying the Rosary daily to fight temptation and evil. When developing this part of your life, start small and let it grow as able. In the appendix are instructions on how to pray the Rosary and the Divine Mercy Chaplet.

WE MUST DRAW UP A BATTLE PLAN.

READ YOUR BIBLE:

Scripture is the Word of God. 2 Timothy 3:16-17 says "All scripture is inspired by God and is useful for teaching, for refutation, for correction, and for training in righteousness, so that one who belongs to God may be competent, equipped for every good work."

CULTIVATE HUMILITY:

Virtues help combat the seven deadly sins and as St. Augustine once said, "Humility is the foundation of all the other virtues hence, in the soul in which this virtue does not exist there cannot be any other virtue except in mere appearance." Because humility is the pursuit of truth, it will help us conquer all the devil's lies.

Now that we've established who our enemy is, looked at his tactics, introduced our weapons, and outlined a core battle plan, it's time to tackle the first capital sin and the first big lie.

CHAPTER 4:
PRIDE

The BIG LIE: YOU CAN HAVE A FULFILLING AND SAVING IDENTITY INDEPENDENT OF GOD.

In 1997, the year I was ordained, the movie *The Devil's Advocate* was released. In it, a proud young southern lawyer, who has never lost a case, is recruited by a high-powered New York City law firm. The head of the firm, a man named John Milton, turns out to be the devil himself, wanting the young lawyer to help bring the Antichrist into the world. The whole story is a study of the destructive ability of pride. From the pride of the devil, who believes he can actually beat God, to the pride of the young lawyer whose desire for the limelight destroys everyone around him. The very last words spoken in the film, "Vanity, definitely my favorite sin" sum up the movie well.

Pride stems from the big lie that we don't need God. It is an unrealistic or disproportionate view of oneself as being equal to God or capable of replacing Him. "Ego non serviam" or "I will not serve" are the words often attributed to the devil as he turned his back on God. Because pride rules the devil for all eternity, he believes he is God's equivalent and can conquer Him. So now he wages a futile war he cannot win, deceived by the lie that he can have a fulfilling and eternally salvific identity independent of God. This is the same lie we believe when we let pride enter our lives.

Pride is the mother of all sin and gives birth to a legion of other sins. It distorts truth, just like the devil does when he tries to manipulate us by tempting us to sin. To get an understanding of how he does this, we must ask ourselves, like Pontius Pilate asks during his interrogation of Jesus in the Gospel of John,

"What is truth?"

There are two types: objective truth and subjective truth. Objective truth is accurate by its own merit, is based on facts, and can be proved easily. For example, it is objectively true that a Brussels sprout is a vegetable. I can call it a fruit, a meat, a fish, or a wagon wheel, but that doesn't change the fact that it *is* a vegetable. Subjective truth is individual and based on opinions and perspective. It relies on one's feelings, likes, dislikes, and perceptions. If I say, "Brussels sprouts are delicious," that is subjectively true. It is my truth but not necessarily correct for everyone else.

In John 14:6, Jesus says, "I am the way, the truth, and the life. No one comes to the Father except through me." Objective truth is bound in God Himself because He is the Creator of all things. Since God is love, we can count on His truth not being subject to selfish whims and desires. It is good and leads to good because He is good.

The devil works to confuse this. He tempts us to believe that objective truth is instead subjective, and that subjective truth can be objective. This is the lie he told Adam and Eve in the garden. He manipulated truth by convincing them that what God told them was subjective and that the pleasing look of the fruit meant it was objectively good. This first temptation was packaged in pride, "You will be like gods." It distorted the truth of how good they had it, leading them to ultimately choose death and sin.

All sin is built on this same essential lie, that you are God's equal (or superior), if God exists at all. Most of us don't parade around saying, "Hi! I'm God." (If you do, you may want to contact your local mental health provider.) Even though most of us don't *think* we are God, we are still tempted to make ourselves a god. It comes in the form of the rationalizations we use to cave to sin, and it allows pride to worm into our souls.

For example, you may know that sex outside of marriage is against God's plan for you, but buy the devil's temptation and rationalize your choices. You may tell yourself that you are an adult or old enough to make your own choices. You may say that premarital sex is okay if you love each other, or that pornography is normal, or that masturbation is healthy. You may think you aren't harming anyone else or worry you will lose your significant other if you don't give yourself to them. Buying any of this reasoning and knowing that sex is pleasurable, puts you in a compromising position. We will discuss this more in the chapter on lust, but the point is, if you know God's plan for human sexuality, but rationalize your way around it, you believe your plan is greater than His. This would make you God's equal or superior, which is the big lie of pride.

Pride also distorts identity. It directs us to see people, including ourselves, in a warped and twisted way. Instead of seeing people as children made in the holy image of God, pride allows us to conceal our inherent dignity and integrity. With this fact obscured, we can easily justify unholy actions. We are led to see ourselves as gods and others as things to be manipulated or used for our own gain.

Unlike some areas of the world, in America we possess a freedom to form our own identities. Our culture not only accepts pride, but celebrates it, even to the point of having entire movements devoted to it. We are told that we can form a fulfilling identity outside of, and independent of, God. But the truth is that we have all been designed with a longing for our Creator and can't have a fulfilling life without Him. If we don't allow God to fill that space, we will attempt to satisfy it with other things like pleasure, sex, greed, over-consumption, etc.

When these ultimately fail, because they all will, pride tells us to numb the emptiness with addictions of all kinds. Pride is a dead end that will never get us where we want to go.

Because it distorts identity, the person caught in pride must also try to change reality to fit their lies. This is a fool's game – no one can do this. The best they can do is force others through pressure, law, and persecution to accept the false reality they've created. The proud person cannot allow alternative realities to exist or theirs is proved wrong. Truth, bound in the Catholic faith, becomes the supreme enemy, and a God who gives us objective truth cannot be allowed to exist.

When we see ourselves with this kind of power, it leads us to the ultimate act of pride - believing we can mold God into whatever image suits our desires, our subjective truth, and our whims. Someone suffering from pride will have a "*my god*" in place of God. Their god is made in their likeness and image, condones their behaviors, despises their opposition, is tolerant of their reality and hates any reality opposed to theirs. Their god sees them as essentially flawless, and those with other opinions as "haters" and "intolerant." Because the proud must form gods in their own image to make their deceit plausible, idolatry is the powertrain behind pride and its deceits.

Idolatry is when we put other things in God's place and give those things more significance than they deserve. We worship idols because subconsciously we believe we can control them, manipulate them, and get the desired results we want. But as Archbishop Charles Chaput remarks in his book, *Things Worth Dying For*, these gods are greedy and far more demanding than the true God. He points out that pagan idols are presented with their arms outstretched to receive – they demand our time, energy, and money, and their thirst has no fulfillment. What a contrast to Jesus who stretches out His arms to give us His life on the cross!

Among the pantheon of gods in our society, fewer have more hold over youth than sports and other organized activities. These gods grab tremendous amounts of time, even seizing for themselves the time supposed to be dedicated to family and church. If I had a dime for every time a parent made the excuse that their child could not come to Mass, parish youth events, sacramental prep, or anything having to do with faith because of some sporting event, I could buy a nice meal at a five-star restaurant and leave a magnanimous tip. Each time those things are chosen over God, an essential lesson is taught - this god is more important and beneficial than the true God. This unspoken lesson reduces God to something that is "fit in" rather than central. Woe to the priest that points this out. No one likes being told they are engaged in idolatry.

The sooner we learn that our idols fall short, the better. None of them will live up to their hype nor can they return our investment. Pride blinds us to this and keeps us pursuing idols hoping for the self-satisfaction we desire. It hides the fact that these gods don't care if they bankrupt us, destroy our health, or make our souls fit for Hell by alluring us with their false promises. The devil cackles as we allow pride to swallow us whole, but if we take up the weapons God has given us, we may get the last laugh.

Your main defense against pride is to cultivate humility because humility is the antidote to pride. On multiple occasions in the Gospels, Jesus tells us to humble ourselves so that he may exalt us.

Unlike what some people think, humility is not a holy self-loathing or perpetually beating yourself up over your faults, sins, and failings. That is self-deprecation. Humility is the pursuit of truth about who you are and who God is. It entails being honest about our sinfulness, faults, and limitations, but using that awareness to love God more, not hate ourselves. When we are humble, we recognize our gifts, talents, and abilities, but we know those ultimately come from God, and that we are nothing without Him. Pursuing this understanding is key. Humility keeps us from pride and ultimately despair, which blinds us from knowing who we truly are. When we know who we are and who God is, we have our scope focused on our vulnerabilities and become skilled at fighting off temptation.

The first step to gaining humility is to refute the first temptation and acknowledge that you and I are not gods. We are not all-powerful or all-knowing, and the realm of what we have control over is very small. Nothing we do will ever change this fact.

The second key is to acknowledge that God is the one true God who has revealed Himself to us through the Scriptures and His Church. Recognizing this allows us to see the emptiness of the idols we have fashioned. It enables us to surrender our pretend lordship and submit to the Lordship of Christ by putting God at the center. In humility, we acknowledge God is God, and that He knows what we need and what is good for us better than we do. We can then pursue God, who yearns for an eternal relationship of mutual love with us.

How do we pursue Him? Jesus gives us the answer in John 8:31-32, "If you remain truly in my word you will remain my disciples, and you will know the truth and the truth will set you free." Here, Jesus is telling us that the weapon we must immerse ourselves in is Holy Scripture. This pursuit of truth is essential for doing battle with the devil's temptation to pride.

When we have the proper relationship with God, Him as God and us as His humble children, we become aware of just how little we know. This is good! It encourages us to pursue the truth – to pursue Christ, who said "I am the way, the truth, and the life" (John 14:6). When you are reading Sacred Scripture, it is imperative to look to the proper translator of the truths contained there – the Church. This is extremely important! The devil can use your reading of Scripture against you by manipulating you to interpret it through the prism of your own biases, fears, and desires. It can sometimes be hard to let go of the god you've created, and easy to mold the Scriptures into something comfortable. We cannot cherry-pick Scriptures to justify lies. The humble person allows the Scriptures to speak objective truth and for God to form him or her into who He asks us to be.

When we read the Bible, we should ask the Holy Spirit for wisdom and knowledge. In asking for these gifts, we are humbly admitting that our own intellectual faculties fall short. We need God's grace to come into a deeper knowledge of Him. This makes sense if you think about it. In my dating years, I relied on my girlfriend to reveal who she was to me. I couldn't have figured her out without her allowing me access, and vice-versa. The same can be said for the friendships I have developed over the years. Many times, we only see what others are willing to show us, and others only see what we are willing to show them. The one exception to this is our relationship with God, who knows us better than we know ourselves. When we pursue a relationship with our Creator, not only do we come to know God better, but through his grace, we come to know ourselves better too.

As we learn uncomfortable things about ourselves, we learn where we need to change and grow. We take these sins to the confessional and allow the sacramental grace Christ gives us in Confession to heal our wounds and help us grow in humility and truth. When God reveals the gifts and abilities He has given us, we should ask God for the wisdom and prudence to exercise these. It's easy to misappropriate talents and use them for the wrong ends, so we should ask God how he intends for us to utilize these gifts.

BATTLE PLAN TO CONQUER PRIDE

> **HUMILITY DRIVES AWAY SATAN AND KEEPS THE GRACES AND GIFTS OF THE HOLY SPIRIT SAFE WITHIN US."**
>
> St. Francis de Sales

The devil hates humility and is the personification of pride. Humility is as foreign and dangerous to him as poisons are to us. When we immerse ourselves in Holy Scripture and cultivate humility, we have sharp weapons to battle pride. Here are some other suggestions that will help you to squash pride in your life:

1. **REFER** to The Core Battle Plan (Chapter 3).

2. **LOOK** to the saints, the great cloud of witnesses, and their experiences in cultivating humility. St. Augustine, St. Francis of Assisi, and St. Ignatius of Loyola struggled with humility and have amazing conversion stories. Ask the saints to intercede for you so you learn, as they did, the path to humility.

3. **STUDY** the life of the Blessed Mother, the best picture of humility we have. She is a prime example of how obedience to God's will is a natural outcome of humility. Ask her to intercede for you.

CONSIDER consecrating yourself to Jesus through Mary. Nothing builds humility quite like knowing every good work you do is no longer yours.

 READ about the apostles of Jesus whose ambitions got in the way of humility. Jesus repeatedly reminded them to humble themselves.

 PRAY the following prayer:

My Lord and My God,

Release me from the blindness of pride.

Release me from the enslavement to the gods and idols I have made.

Release me from the deceit which hampers my path to You.

Open my eyes to see the truth of who You are and who I am.

Open my mind to see the beauty and truth that is You.

Open my heart to humbly accept You and seek You above all things.

Draw me to You in truth so that I may be the child of God You have created me to be.

Send Your holy angels to defend me from the attacks and deceits of the devil so that I may walk in truth.

Amen

> **IT WAS PRIDE THAT CHANGED THE ANGELS TO DEVILS, IT IS HUMILITY THAT MAKES MEN AS ANGELS."**
>
> St. Augustine

CHAPTER 5:
LUST

YOU ARE NO MORE THAN AN ANIMAL.

When the devil convinces you to be your own god, you gain the ability to create your own moral compass. You can fashion morality from noble concepts like equality and world peace, or from a celebrity in your social media feed. The options for what is "right" are endless and completely up to you! It may sound like a dream, but it's actually a nightmare.

Over the years there has been a lot of discussion about who or what a human is. With the introduction of atheistic evolution, where humanity is reduced to a highly-intelligent animal, the idea that there is an objective morality tied to objective truth is seen as outdated and oppressive. If you see yourself as "one of the beasts," passion becomes your driving force. Animals are driven by their sexual desire. They spread their seed like a rapper throwing 'Benjamins' in a music video, never worrying about the consequences – so why can't we? If we are just mammals, how can we be expected to reign in our natural sexual appetites when our distant 'cousins' can't?

This attitude became widespread in the 1960s with The Sexual Revolution plague. During this time, people were encouraged to express their sexuality as they saw fit, without caring about the repercussions. Decades later, much to the delight of the devil, we now have a society absolutely saturated with sex. Sex has infiltrated every form of entertainment and is virtually inescapable. The devil knows that one of the easiest pathways to separate us from God is to turn God's gift of sexuality against us, and that is exactly what he's done. Our Lady told St. Jacinta Marto, one of the visionaries of Fatima, that more souls go to hell because of sins of the flesh than for any other reason. Because the sins of the flesh are so effective at aiding the devil's mission, it's important to spend some considerable time here.

The devil sees no inherent beauty, dignity, and integrity in the human person. He persuades us to compartmentalize and degrade ourselves. He convinces us to believe what the abortion supporters shout from the rooftops, "My body, my choice."

When you believe his lie that you know best how to use your body, lust sits down in the driver's seat. And trust me, your new chauffeur isn't taking you down Sexual Dignity & Respect Lane. Mr. Lust is a creepy dude dressed in a disordered desire for sexual pleasure that divorces sex from any Divine design. He sees the body as a pleasure playground open 24/7. When lust is behind the wheel, sexual acts become nothing more than a means to an end because you're just an animal chasing after the chemical rush of an orgasm. When sex is drained of Divine purpose, how one achieves that neurotransmitter hit is irrelevant.

Nowhere is this more evident than in masturbation and pornography. These two are often presented as harmless because they seemingly involve no one else; however, they are both extremely damaging to our souls, and the lessons learned through use have lasting effects. When we misuse our sexuality, we are distorting something beautiful that God created. God designed sex to be enjoyed between a married couple open to life. When we participate outside of this context, we are separating the physical act from its God-given purpose and making it all about bodily pleasure.

In masturbation, you teach yourself that you are nothing more than an object for physical gratification – essentially, you dehumanize yourself.

Because fantasies often accompany self-pleasure, we bring whoever we are fantasizing about into our sordid act and mentally rape them for our own ends. Many of you have been taught that masturbation is healthy and normal. That is a lie. It is not healthy (and shouldn't be normal) to objectify ourselves.

The accompaniment of pornography amplifies these negative effects because it extends that objectification to others. Pornography currently permeates our media and the devil, like society, wants you to believe that it is acceptable and safe. Those are also lies. When we view and treat others as objects for our pleasure, it strips away their human dignity. While watching porn, the viewer becomes the master of someone who won't say "no" to any depravities he or she can entertain. Besides having their self-respect stripped away, many of the 'actors' in porn videos aren't fully-consenting participants - they are in fact, abuse victims. Did you know porn fuels the human trafficking industry? When you consume the 'goods' you are driving demand and creating a need for increased supply. In this case, the supply is people – other sons and daughters of God.

Research also shows that pornography harms YOU. It is addictive, rewires your brain, and can prevent you from being mentally capable of creating the bonds necessary for a mutually-loving relationship. Porn makes relationships completely irrelevant by teaching us to divorce sexuality from its relational bonds. Over time, porn users, just like with other drugs, develop a tolerance, and need different stimulation to get "a hit." Because of this, the adult porn industry now fuels the child porn industry, and subsequently child sex trafficking. Nothing is more horrific than the sexual abuse of an innocent child. Unlike what the devil tries to tell us, pornography and masturbation are anything but victimless crimes. They leave a wake of destruction for everyone involved and cheapen the holiness of God's creation.

The truth is that we are all made in the image and likeness of God and our bodies are temples of the Holy Spirit. St. Paul tells us to "Flee from sexual immorality. All other sins a person commits are outside the body, but whoever sins sexually, sins against their own body. Do you not know that your bodies are temples of the Holy Spirit, who is in you, whom you have received from God? You are not your own; you were bought at a price. Therefore, honor God with your bodies" (1 Corinthians 6:18-20).

The devil tempts us to treat others as a board game to sate our passions instead of as temples of the Lord. Even if someone is willing (or wanting) you to pass "Go" and collect $200, you are still bound to uphold their dignity and integrity. Ripping sexual acts out of marriage or seeing how far you can go before it's "too much," desecrates both temples involved. We will always struggle with temptation because of concupiscence; however, we are given the graces necessary to keep our bodies, minds, and souls free from the sins of the flesh through Christ.

At your baptism you were washed in water and anointed by the Holy Spirit through Sacred Chrism. The entirety of who you are was set apart for God's use. Your body, in all of its parts, is as St. John Paul II reminds us, a sacrament by which others come to know the love of God. You were made for self-giving love, not for self-centered lust.

Most of what the Church declares as sinful regarding human sexuality is considered normal by society. This causes confusion. St. John Paul II wrote a great piece called *Theology of the Body* that gives a thorough explanation of the teachings of the Church regarding sexuality and family. It is far too often ignored, while society functions as the primary Sex Ed teacher.

The Church also recognizes how hard the struggle against the flesh can be, especially when these behaviors are habitual, or someone is caught in an addiction. In 1975, the Congregation for the Doctrine of Faith released *Humana Persona*. Here they explain that factors such as the immaturity of adolescents, psychological imbalances, and habits can influence people's behavior and diminish "the deliberate character of the act and bringing about a situation whereby subjectively there may not always be serious fault" (9.4) Here, the Congregation is not diminishing the seriousness of these sins or absolving a person to continue to masturbate or use porn, but instead they are recognizing the hold these can have on someone who is enslaved. Pastors are instructed to "exercise patience and goodness; but they are not allowed to render God's commandments null, nor to unreasonably reduce people's responsibility" (10.8).

The Church takes a stance of recognizing that these actions are sinful by nature and have grave consequences, but also realizing sexual addictions can be a titanic struggle. Just like Jesus was unwavering in his stance on evil, but merciful towards individuals, priests should follow in the Lord's footsteps when dealing with people on these matters. Similar advice is found in the *Catechism* in paragraph 2352.

It's important to recognize that no one is ever "too far gone." The sacramental grace of Confession and instruction from shepherds can guide you past these types of addictions. If you find yourself trapped, be assured you are not alone, and as with all sin, Christ wants you to be free.

YOUR WEAPONS TO FIGHT LUST

Our most powerful weapon in this fight against lust is the same as the previous chapter: humility. Humility is a search for the truth, so it leads us to dismiss the devil's big lie that we are mere animals who cannot control our passions. It confirms that we are made in the image and likeness of God and that there is an inherent dignity in all of us that must be respected.

Humility leads us to understand that we are temples of the Holy

Spirit, set aside for God's use, by virtue of our baptism. Hence, we treat our bodies with respect as we would something holy. I use this example often. Let's say you were to see me gardening and I was using a chalice from Mass as a shovel. I would imagine you would stop me and reprimand me for doing so. What if I were to reply, "Do you hate chalices or gardening?!" I would imagine you would say, "No, I have nothing against gardening, but you are using a chalice to scoop dirt. That is not right!" In fact, it would be a sacrilege and you would be correct. Just because I *could* use the chalice for something other than Mass does not mean that I *should,* or that the use wouldn't be sinful. By the same token, the Catholic Church does not believe that human sexuality is evil. We see it as good, in fact, we see it as holy. There is a right way to use this gift that is in union with God's intent. Humility opens our eyes to see these things and leads us to the other great weapon against Satan in the fight against lust: chastity.

Lust is the disordering of human sexuality, and chastity, which is refraining from sexual activity outside of marriage, is the opposite. The *Catechism* tells us that "Sexuality…becomes personal and truly human when it is integrated into the relationship of one person to another, in the complete and lifelong mutual gift of a man and a woman" (CCC 2337). The virtue of chastity gives us the tools to order our own sexuality into God's intention and away from the worldly perception that our bodies are subject to our biological passions.

A virtue is a Godly discipline by which we are given the ability to temper and learn to positively choose what is good and holy. Chastity is a virtue we build choice by choice. The *Catechism* tells us that "Chastity includes an *apprenticeship in self-mastery* which is a training in human freedom. The alternative is clear: either man governs his passions and finds peace, or he lets himself be dominated by them and becomes unhappy. 'Man's dignity therefore requires him to act out of conscious and free choice, as moved and drawn in a personal way from within, and not by blind impulses in himself or by mere external constraint. Man gains such dignity when, ridding himself of all slavery to the passions, he presses forward to his goal by freely choosing what is good and, by his diligence and skill, effectively secures for himself the means suited to this end'" (CCC 2339). Read that again.

Contrary to what society says about us being hopelessly enslaved to our passions, God gives us His grace to overcome these, so that we may truly love as He loves. To love as God loves, is to leave no room for turning another person (or ourselves) into an object for self-gratification. You don't need to be a slave of sin or your passions. Chastity is filed under the greater cardinal virtue of temperance (CCC 2341), which is the virtue of self-mastery. This means not becoming lord of our own life, but by the grace of God, subject our passions to our souls. This type of self-mastery helps us grow in strength.

Consider this example: In weightlifting, the person grows muscle mass because they challenge what the muscles can do. The challenge tears the muscle, and the healing process makes muscles grow. If the muscle is not challenged, it will atrophy and start to shrink in mass and strength. The human intellect grows when it is challenged through study. If the mind goes unchallenged, the person loses the ability to grow their mind and their intellectual capacity dissolves.

What is true for the body and mind is also true for the soul. Through self-mastery, guided by the grace of God, we grow in holiness and can successfully see the devil's handiwork and refute it.

WHEN WE DO NOT ENGAGE IN TEMPERANCE, WE GROW WEAKER IN OUR ABILITY TO RESIST SIN AND WE ARE AN EASY TARGET FOR THE DEVIL.

BATTLE PLAN TO CONQUER LUST

> "FASTING CLEANSES THE SOUL, RAISES THE MIND, SUBJECTS ONE'S FLESH TO THE SPIRIT, RENDERS THE HEART CONTRITE AND HUMBLE, SCATTERS THE CLOUDS OF CONCUPISCENCE, QUENCHES THE FIRE OF LUST, AND KINDLES THE TRUE LIGHT OF CHASTITY."
>
> St. Augustine

As we established earlier in this chapter, humility, chastity, and temperance should be cultivated to fight lust. Here are some suggestions for establishing these virtues:

1. **REFER** to The Core Battle Plan (Chapter 3).

2. Like St. Augustine suggests in the quote above, **INCORPORATE** fasting in your efforts. When you deny your body the food that it wants, you grow in spiritual strength. You prove to yourself that you are not controlled by your physical desires and the strength of your will grows.

3 When the mountain in front of you seems too high to climb, focus on taking one right step at a time. **AIM** to make your next choice a positive one. Then do it again the time after that, and the time after that, etc. Just focus on doing the next right thing.

4 When a temptation presents itself, **MAKE** a holy choice. Instead of choosing to click on the pornographic website, decide to pray the Rosary and ask the Blessed Mother for assistance to resist the urge to sin.

5 **PRACTICE** learning custody of the eyes. Do not allow the immodesty of others to become an excuse for your sins. You control what you choose to place your eyes on and the thoughts you allow yourself to entertain. If your eyes or thoughts start to linger on something unholy, picture Jesus Christ on the Cross and meditate on His Passion.

6 **TURN** to Jesus for His mercy in the Sacrament of Reconciliation. Using Confession in the ongoing battle with the desires of the flesh helps us master such passions.

7 **DON'T** put yourself in compromising positions. For example, if you know you will struggle being alone with someone and making a holy choice, choose dates that allow you to surround yourself with other people. Dating people with similar values helps immensely.

8 PRAY the following prayer:

My Lord and My God,

Through Your own incarnation You opened wide the restoration of our bodies from slaves of sins to masters of our passions.

We ask, O Lord, that You give us the strength to exercise the virtues of humility, chastity, and temperance, so that we may respect, and see as holy, the temples of the Holy Spirit that we and our neighbors are called to be.

Help us to govern our passions so that our bodies and souls may give You eternal praise.

In Your most holy name we pray.

Amen

PRAY AND

> "LUST IS THE LOVE OF THE PLEASURES THAT ARE CONTRARY TO PURITY. NO SINS, MY CHILDREN, RUIN AND DESTROY A SOUL SO QUICKLY AS THIS SHAMEFUL SIN; IT SNATCHES US OUT OF THE HANDS OF THE GOOD GOD AND HURLS US LIKE A STONE INTO AN ABYSS OF MIRE AND CORRUPTION. ONCE PLUNGED INTO THIS MIRE, WE CANNOT GET OUT, WE MAKE A DEEPER HOLE IN IT EVERY DAY, WE SINK LOWER AND LOWER. THEN WE LOSE THE FAITH, WE LAUGH AT THE TRUTHS OF RELIGION, WE NO LONGER SEE HEAVEN, WE DO NOT FEAR HELL. O MY CHILDREN! HOW MUCH ARE THEY TO BE PITIED WHO GIVE WAY TO THIS PASSION."
>
> St. John Vianney

LISTEN FOR GOD'S VOICE

CHAPTER 6:
GREED

The BIG LIE

HAPPINESS IS FOUND IN THE ACCUMULATION OF WORLDLY GOODS.

One of the top movies in 1987 was the movie *Wall Street*. The main characters of the film are Gordon Gekko, a corporate raider who disassembles corporations for money, and a young protégé named Bud Fox, who ends up outwitting his master through insider trading. Both characters are shameless in their pursuit of money and power. At one point, Gordon gives the following speech, "The point is, ladies and gentlemen, that greed – for lack of a better word – is good. Greed is right. Greed works. Greed clarifies, cuts through, and captures the essence of the evolutionary spirit. Greed in all its forms, greed for life, for money, for love, for knowledge, has marked the upward surge of mankind." Sounds like a great guy to hang out with, huh?

Greed is a disproportionate desire for the goods of this world. When it comes to greed, the devil has some lies to sell. He tells you that security and happiness are found through the collection of things, that God's plans will not satisfy, and that giving, instead of taking for yourself, will leave you destitute and unfulfilled. He tells you that consumption and accumulation are equivalent to progress, and that the more you have, the happier and more respected, feared, and liked, you will be. He whispers that you *have* to have the latest iPhone because it will bring you the joy that you *deserve*. Greed confuses want with need, and luxury with necessity. It tells us that life beyond the grave is uncertain, so we must live it up now. Greed willingly surrenders the everlasting joy of eternity with our Lord, for a sweet sportscar and a beach house in the present.

Although it is easy for us to associate greed with people like Gordon Gekko or the wealthy upper class, greed does not require someone to be a robber baron or have a seven-figure salary. Greed clings to anyone who ruthlessly follows the path towards accumulation of goods, and it is much more pervasive in our society than most people think.

Greed first appears early in our lives. If you've ever babysat, you know exactly what I'm talking about. I was in my tweens/teens when my last four siblings were born within a span of five years. I had A LOT of exposure to toddlers. (We joke that they scared me into the priesthood.) Toddlers have the mentality, "What's mine is mine, what's yours is mine, and what's broken is yours." Watching them is like a tutorial on greed, gluttony, and envy. I would witness them hoard toys and steal them from each other, only to use them for a few seconds before getting bored.

As we get older, greed isn't as obvious. Most of us don't go over to a friend's house and stockpile the Oreos in their pantry or sneak off in their new Corvette. Around the time you start using the big kid potty, people expect you to behave better. Although we don't act the same way we did when we were toddlers, we covertly share the same sentiments. Many times, greed shows up as consumerism or overworking. It whispers that your time, energy, and resources are yours and are there primarily to serve your own wants and needs.

One of the devil's favorite tricks is to convince us our sins aren't really sins. He makes it easy to come up with a myriad of excuses to justify our greed, because it's extremely hard to fight, let alone repent for, sins whose existence we deny. If you take an honest look at society, you'll see that greed is everywhere.

In 21st century America, we live in a consumerist society. Many of us, like Dave Ramsey says, "spend money we don't have, to buy things we don't need, to impress people we don't like." According to CNBC, the average American has $90,460 in debt, and an article from Credit Ninja shares data that young Americans are falling into more debt faster than previous generations.

Thanks to credit cards, it's easy to spend money we don't have, and stores are open every day of the week to encourage frivolous spending. The "blue laws" of my childhood, which aimed to keep businesses closed and Sunday as a day of rest, are long gone. While there are still a handful of establishments that close for the Sabbath, like Chick-fil-A (a.k.a. "God's Chicken"), Sundays now largely look like every other day. We had to greedily take the time allotted for worship and family to pursue our own desires. This change didn't happen overnight though. First, the culture seized the afternoons and evenings, reducing the Lord's day to the Lord's morning. Eventually, society lost respect for the morning, and God's time was shortened to sixty minutes (many sports leagues and companies make it almost impossible for people to even get that)! The pursuit of the worldly has largely trumped the pursuit of the Divine, and rather than receiving a rejuvenating rest on the Sabbath, greed has virtually wiped out the Third Commandment. Many will pat themselves on the back for getting in that hour for Mass, but God didn't say, "Keep holy one hour on the Sabbath." (Insert mic drop here.)

Besides taking our time and energy, greed also commandeers our resources. In 1 Timothy 6:10, St. Paul tells us that the love of money is the root of all evil. Its unrelenting pursuit can be blinding, directing us to either an extravagant lifestyle or a miserly one. Both of those lead to separation from God, just like in the Parable of the Rich Man and Lazarus in Luke 16:19-31. The rich man, with greed in his heart, ignores the needs of a poor man named Lazarus who lies slowly dying at his doorstop. Go read those verses to see where he winds up. Let's just say he's not sipping piña coladas in a hammock with a heavenly view.

For the record, the desire for worldly things is not always bad. The *Catechism* teaches that, "The sensitive appetite leads us to desire pleasant things we do not have, e.g., the desire to eat when hungry or to warm ourselves when we are cold. These desires are good in themselves; but often they exceed the limits of reason and drive us to covet unjustly what is not ours and belongs to another or is

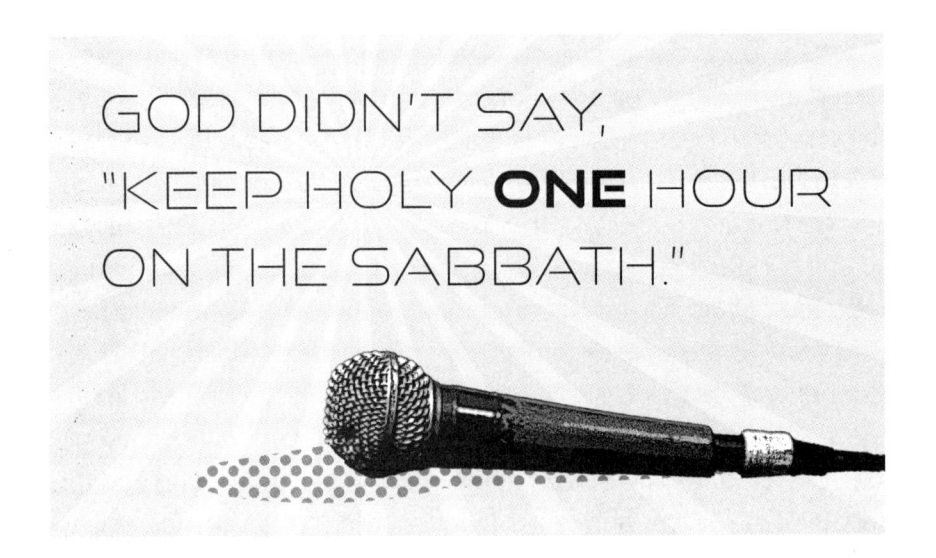

> GOD DIDN'T SAY, "KEEP HOLY **ONE** HOUR ON THE SABBATH."

owed to him. The tenth commandment forbids greed and the desire to amass earthly goods without limit. It forbids *avarice* arising from a passion for riches and their attendant power. It also forbids the desire to commit injustice by harming our neighbor in his temporal goods. (CCC 2535-2536).

X. Thou shalt not covet

When greed gets to the point mentioned above, it blinds us to the needs of others and makes us indifferent. It may lead us to refrain from (or severely curtail) tithing, or to refrain from helping those in need.

As we wrap up this chapter, it's worth it to note that greed likes to hang out with a couple other capital sins. Greed is a child of pride. Pride tells us we can find an eternally fulfilling identity independent of God, and greed lines up the idols for us to pursue. Greed also usually goes hand-in-hand with envy, and it's the powertrain for gluttony. Like all the capital sins, greed leaves us empty by making a promise it cannot keep. It cannot ever bring lasting happiness. Actor Jim Carrey once said, "I think everyone should get rich and famous and do everything they ever dreamed of, so they can see that it's not the answer."

YOUR WEAPONS TO FIGHT GREED

Our greatest weapon to fight greed (insert drumroll please) is.... you guessed it, HUMILITY! You're smart young Catholics, so I know you're seeing a pattern here. St. Augustine, in his *Confessions*, talks about how he pursued worldly things, finding each one more unfulfilling than the last, until finally he understood "Our hearts are restless until they rest in Thee." Because humility is bound in truth, it helps us to see that the things of this world will never satisfy the hole that was designed to be filled only by Christ. It is through seeking Christ that we find fulfillment. Humility sees that the proper use of our time and energy is not to accumulate things, but to learn to love as God loves.

It also teaches us to recognize what the Scriptures repeatedly say, "All good things come from God" (James 1:17, 1 Chronicles 16:11-12, Psalm 16:2). In our Christian faith, most think stewardship is about money. It's not. Stewardship is about using the time, energy, and resources given to us in a way that helps build up the Kingdom – not to merely suit our own ends. Stewardship helps us recognize our part in God's unfolding plan of salvation and connects us to His will.

There are three great tools in our Faith to drive this home: fasting, abstinence, and almsgiving. You may be familiar with these concepts from Lent, but they are not *only* for the Lenten season. Each teaches us a right ordering of our passions so that we do not become enslaved to them.

In fasting and abstinence, we learn the right use of worldly goods. We typically attach these concepts to food and drink, but the principle can apply to many things. For example, you could fast/abstain from your endless need to be entertained. This could be as simple as leaving the radio off in the car and praying a Rosary instead or turning off your phone at a certain time each evening. Fasting and abstinence help us to rightly order our day and break our slavish dependence on the things of this world.

Almsgiving is giving money to those in need. It forces us to see money as a tool to help others and not something to be hoarded or squandered. It forces us to see beyond ourselves and learn to love others as God asks us to. Almsgiving also helps us to be benevolent masters of our wealth instead of our wealth mastering us. Instead of money being something we love, it becomes a servant to Christ and is seen as a tool to be generously used.

The Scriptures themselves also give us an antidote to combat greed. It comes in the thanksgiving offering/sacrifice (also known as the tithe), and the active concern and charity that was supposed to be shown to those in need. The tithe was used to support those whose lives were dedicated to the service of God and His people, as well as the poor and needy. Besides tithing, the people of Israel were also forbidden to go back for a second round of harvesting. Whatever was missed the first time around was to be left for the poor and needy (see Leviticus 19:9 and 23:22, Deuteronomy 24:19). This act of generosity was intended to mirror the generosity God had first shown them. We are called to the same type of sacrificial offerings.

BATTLE PLAN TO CONQUER GREED

> "EARTHLY RICHES ARE LIKE THE REED. ITS ROOTS ARE SUNK IN THE SWAMP AND ITS EXTERIOR, IS FAIR TO BEHOLD BUT INSIDE, IT IS HOLLOW. IF A MAN LEANS ON SUCH A REED, IT WILL SNAP OFF AND PIERCE HIS SOUL."
>
> St. Anthony of Padua

In Matthew 6:19-21 we are told, "Do not store up for yourselves treasures on earth, where moth and decay destroy, and thieves break in and steal. But store up treasures in heaven, where neither moth nor decay destroys, nor thieves break in and steal. For where your treasure is, there also will your heart be." Therefore, our battle plan for greed is designed to help us store treasures in heaven, so that our hearts can follow.

1 **REFER** to The Core Battle Plan (Chapter 3).

2 **PRACTICE** fasting, abstinence, and almsgiving.

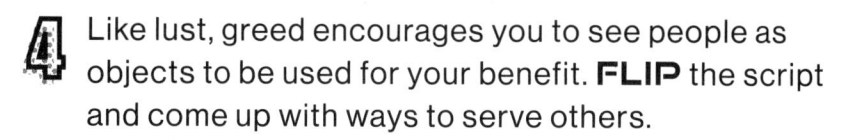

3 Since greed blinds you to the needs of others, **FIND** ways to show concern and charity for the needy.

4 Like lust, greed encourages you to see people as objects to be used for your benefit. **FLIP** the script and come up with ways to serve others.

5 **TITHE.** In Malachi 3:8-12, to withhold the tithe was likened to stealing from God.

6 **AIM** to be a good steward of your time, energy, and resources. Make sure you are not using them merely for your own wants and needs.

7 **PRAY** this prayer:

My Lord and My God,

You have made us out of love so that we may learn to love.

Forgive us for the many times we hoarded Your gifts or squandered them.

Forgive us for placing our trust in worldly things and not in You.

Help us to detach from a disordered love of wealth, and with thankful hearts make a sacrifice pleasing to You, that acknowledges Your goodness in our lives.

Free us from greed in all of its deceits.

Amen

CHAPTER 7:
ENVY

The BIG LIE

OTHER PEOPLE'S SUCCESS AND POSSESSIONS ARE A DANGER TO YOU.

William Shakespeare, in his great tragedy *Othello* writes, "O beware my Lord of jealousy, it is the green-eyed monster which doth mock the meat it feeds on" (Act 3, Scene 2). Jealousy and envy are very closely related and cause you to see the admirable traits or good fortunes of others as a detriment to yourself. Although many people use these terms interchangeably, envy is a desire for the possessions of others (also known as coveting), and jealousy is an unpleasant apprehension of rivalry. Both feast on those who harbor them.

Envy is a deadly sin because it destroys everything it touches, divides us into rivals by pitting us against each other, and dehumanizes the parties involved. Envy was likely at the very heart of Lucifer's downfall from Heaven because he saw the creation of humanity as a threat.

The devil's familiarity with envy allows him to easily use it as a tool against us. His goal is to separate us from God, and because envy can only divide, it works to his advantage when we see each other (and God) as enemies. In fact, even the original temptation in the Garden of Eden was wrapped in envy. He convinced Adam and Eve that God did not want them to have what He has and to know what He knows. Later in Genesis, envy strikes again when it drives Cain to murder his brother Abel.

Even though envy is so damaging to individuals and relationships, we are immersed in it. In the 21st century it has become the "mode of operating" for how to get ahead in both politics and daily life. According to our Western culture, anyone who rises must be brought back down, a concept that is sometimes referred to as "crab mentality."

Apparently if you put one crab in a bucket, it can claw its way out and return to the wild. But something interesting happens if you put a group of them in a bucket together. If one crab tries to escape, the rest of the crabs pull it back into the bucket. The crabs can become so vicious that if one keeps trying to escape, the others gang up on it and may break its claws (or even kill it) to stop it from climbing. Humans sometimes exhibit similar sentiments when someone around them is achieving because they see it as a threat to themselves – which is absolutely absurd!

Just look at the pattern of the rise and collapse of teenage pop stars. Typically, a young man or woman will come on the scene with a few songs that become hits. People begin to make fun of them online as they have every move and word scrutinized. The Paparazzi stalks them, looking for any piece of evidence to destroy the teen. When the scrutiny causes him or her to buckle, envy has claimed its next victim. Was this person's success a threat to anyone? No. But envy causes people to despise the success of others.

We also see this type of behavior in other aspects of our culture. People separate into clans that are deeply suspicious of each other. We divide on race, culture, language, education, socio-economic conditions, location, creed, and a myriad of other categories that stare each other down. This leads to a zero-sum game that leaves people striving for an equality of outcome instead of equality of opportunity. The former is impossible without a higher authority doing the dirty work – insert big government here.

An example of the type of sub-grouping interactions I'm talking about occurred after the U.S. Civil War and the emancipation of slaves.

There was a belief in some sectors of the white community that the success of black people was an endangerment to them. Sounds like some crabs we just talked about, doesn't it?

These human-sized crabs used their claws to set up Jim Crow laws designed to limit the ability of black men and women to succeed. In places where black people did flourish, like in the Greenwood district of Tulsa, Oklahoma, tensions were strong. All that was needed to ignite the flame was a small spark, in this case a young white woman made a false accusation of assault against a young black man and yanked him back into the bucket. Envy reared its ugly head and Greenwood, known as the "Black Wall Street" for its prosperity, burned to the ground. Many of the businesses, homes, and churches were looted by white men. Even the only hospital in the district was destroyed.

A few chapters ago, we established that humans are not merely animals, but with the help of the devil, they sure can act like them sometimes. Envy is a horrific thing and never misses an opportunity. A hundred years later, purveyors of envy now paint all white men and women as inherently racist, no different than those who destroyed Greenwood. Envy never lets good divisive propaganda go to waste.

A lesson to learn here is that envy divides, polarizes, and requires scapegoats. It needs victims and aggressors. Whether it was Hitler using the Jews' post-war success as the reason Germans suffered, or Stalin blaming upper class peasants, known as Kulaks, for the woes of the USSR, stirring up envy makes the tyrants the savior and elimination of the envied group necessary. Sydney J. Harris once said, "History repeats itself, but in such cunning disguise that we never detect the resemblance until the damage is done." You young Catholics know by now who the master of disguise is. We must learn to recognize him when he's staring us in the face.

It's easier to see the destruction that envy does on a grand scale; however, most of the time we struggle with envy on a smaller scale. The harm can be every bit as real, but it can be easier to overlook. Over the years, how many times have you resented a classmate for higher grades or playing time on sports teams, or begrudged coworkers for their promotions and recognition? How many times have we been envious of people in our lives instead of being happy for them? It's easier to resent the groundwork of others instead of analyzing our own shortcomings or subpar effort. This tendency is not just for the laity, I've even seen it in the priesthood. When a brother priest gets a bigger or more prestigious parish, gets named monsignor, etc., the immediate response can be to presume the guy is chummy with the bishop or has the right connections. This type of envy causes Father Crab to resent his brother, look down on his current assignment, and be robbed of his joy. Envy robs everyone of joy.

One of the worst things about envy is that it blinds us to our own God-given gifts and talents. It robs us of the ability to be thankful for what we have and to be genuinely happy for others, while holding us back from our unique call. The examples for how envy can destroy are endless, but the result is always the same – resentment and division. It's time we fight back.

As we've established many times, the devil speaks in lies. Envy doesn't need to be built on facts, only perceptions. The foundation of envy is made up of several lies. First, the devil tells us that the success or state of others must have come because of some type of injustice. Second, the devil says that those who seemingly have it better than we do, do not deserve it. Third, the devil convinces us that we are by nature self-deficient and the only way to even the balance is to seize from others and redistribute to ourselves.

Since all successful lies have a grain of truth, sometimes those who are victorious in worldly matters have gotten such success from unjust means. Sometimes - not always. Sometimes, people are better off because of other people's means. This does not make them inherently evil nor their wealth ill-gotten. Yes, they may not use these advantages well, but whether someone deserves it cannot be discerned most of the time. It is true that we are self-deficient by nature and that we need others and the grace of God to grow in every venue of our lives; however, to believe the only way this can be rectified is to take from others is shortchanging God's grace and leading us to squander our own gifts.

YOUR WEAPONS TO FIGHT ENVY

With envy, it's important to hone your offense. The way we do this is to recognize what the devil is trying to serve us. Envy doesn't need to be built on facts, only perceptions. You may have shown up in the café looking forward to a B.L.T. with crispy bacon, crunchy lettuce, and juicy tomatoes between two perfectly toasted pieces of bread, but here comes the devil with an E.L.T. special on a silver platter. You may perceive it as the classic American staple, but he's substituted one little letter, and now you're munching on Envy, Lies, and Temptation.

Let's take a look at how the evil head chef concocts his specialty. He preheats the envy in our hearts by telling us that the success of another must have come from some type of injustice. He throws the lies together as he whispers that others do not deserve their advantages. Then he bakes in the temptation, telling us the only way to even the balance is to seize from others and redistribute to ourselves. Yummy, eh? But because of that pesky grain of truth, too many people willingly gobble up this poison.

As with all our other battles with the devil, we must begin with the pursuit of truth which can only be found in humility. Regarding envy, humility allows you to see the blessings, abilities, talents, and gifts God has bestowed on you. If you struggle with this, it will be hard to see the positives within yourself. The devil needs us to focus on the negative, so overcoming this is essential.

When you start to give your blessings an honest assessment, it leads you to analyze whether you are using those in the way God wants you to. It will allow you to put the focus on how to use those gifts and talents, instead of wasting time speculating how another got "ahead."

BATTLE PLAN TO CONQUER ENVY

> "THE SOUL THAT LOVES JESUS CHRIST DOES NOT ENVY THE GREAT ONES OF THIS WORLD BUT ONLY THOSE WHO ARE GREATER LOVERS OF JESUS CHRIST."
>
> St. Alphonsus Liguori

To diminish the power of envy in your life, do the following:

1. **REFER** to The Core Battle Plan (Chapter 3).

2. **DO** an honest assessment of God's blessings in your life. Are you using them the way God has called you to?

3 **SPEND** time in Adoration. Spend time before the Blessed Sacrament in prayer, asking God to reveal the gifts, blessings, talents, and abilities He has given to you – then thank God for them.

4 **DEVELOP** a profound sense of gratitude. Before going to bed, after examining your conscience and saying an Act of Contrition, come up with five things you are grateful for. This helps you to develop discipline in looking for God's blessings and action in your lives.

5 At the end of each day, **THINK** about five people or events that you need to bring to God before going to bed. Train your mind to think about how you can assist others, instead of seeing them as a threat.

6 **LOOK** for the good in others and pray for those you are envious of. St. Josemaria Escriva says in his book *The Way*, "Do not say this person annoys me. Think: This person sanctifies me." We can apply this same concept to those we envy. If we pray for them instead, we learn to be a better follower of Christ.

7 **DEVELOP** the theological virtue of charity, also known as love. In the *Catechism of the Catholic Church*, charity is defined as "the theological virtue by which we love God above all things for his own sake, and our neighbor as ourselves for the love of God" (CCC 1822). A heart of love has no room for envy because it doesn't see the good of another as a threat.

8 Every day, **MAKE** the conscious and deliberate effort to see your neighbor not as your competition, but as your brother or sister. Love changes how you perceive people and charity is a discipline we strengthen one choice at a time. When you develop this, you will not engage in the ugly presumption of envy or seek scapegoats for your own shortcomings or problems.

9 **DO NOT ALLOW** the artificial divisions that envy foists on humanity (race, culture, etc.) to become reasons to be suspicious of others. Love is the anti-venom for envy.

> "LOOK AT THE SET OF SENSELESS REASONS THE ENEMY GIVES YOU FOR ABANDONING YOUR PRAYER. 'I HAVE NO TIME'—WHEN YOU ARE CONSTANTLY WASTING IT. 'THIS IS NOT FOR ME.' 'MY HEART IS DRY...'
>
> PRAYER IS NOT A QUESTION OF WHAT YOU SAY OR FEEL, BUT OF LOVE. AND YOU LOVE WHEN YOU TRY HARD TO SAY SOMETHING TO THE LORD, EVEN THOUGH YOU MIGHT NOT ACTUALLY SAY ANYTHING."
>
> St. Josemaría Escrivá

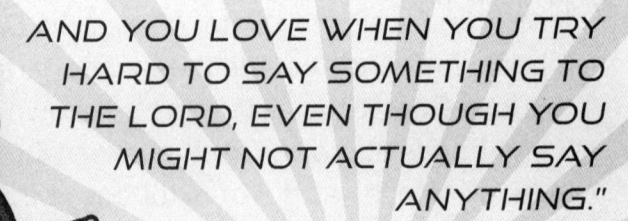

10. **PRAY** this prayer:

My Lord and My God,

I repent of the times I have allowed envy to darken my heart against those I am called to love.

I repent of the times I have allowed human biases to color the way I look at others.

I repent of the times I have seen Your gifts to others as a detriment to me.

I pray that You fill my heart with gratitude for the good in the lives of others and myself.

I pray that You teach me to love so that I seek and support the good of others.

Amen

LOVE IS THE ANTI-VENOM OF ENVY

CHAPTER 8:
GLUTTONY

The BIG LIE

CONTENTMENT COMES FROM CONSUMPTION.

One of the most popular sitcoms of all time is the series called *Friends*. For those not familiar with the show, it focuses on a group of six friends in their twenties, living in New York City. Two or three seasons into its run, a theory arose that each of the main characters, along with the owner of the coffee shop they frequented, represented one of the seven deadly sins. Whether the writers intended that or not, the theory made sense. The person said to represent gluttony was Joey. Once you start watching, you notice that he eats constantly and is obsessed with food.

In an episode from season 10, Joey starts seeing a girl named Sarah who breaks his golden "I don't share food" rule, by eating fries off his plate. He's reluctant to go out with her again but agrees to go on a second date. When their desserts are delivered, Joey is disappointed that his cheesecake has raspberry coulis on top, while his date swoons over the deliciousness of her chocolate torte. Suddenly, Sarah's pager goes off and she excuses herself to make a phone call. Joey then stares longingly at her plate and eventually convinces himself that one little taste is okay. After indulging, he says, "Uh oh" as the camera fades away.

In the next scene, when Sarah returns, Joey's face is covered in chocolate and the plate is empty as he looks at her and says, "I'm not even sorry" with a giant smile on his face. This may make for great comedy, but an attachment like this is not a laughing matter in real life.

Although most people associate gluttony with overeating, that is only part of it. Gluttony includes being overly picky about food and considers when and why a person eats or drinks. The issue is that a glutton cannot say no to the appetites, which is very dangerous to the soul. They battle with temptation and fail to restrain themselves as they mindlessly consume.

Fr. Mike Schmitz, in a video about gluttony, gives the example of binging on a family-sized bag of his favorite chips. The first few bites, he takes in the flavor and savors it, but before he knows it the bag is empty, and he realizes he mindlessly crunched through most of it. How many times have you done something similar?

Even if you don't struggle with food and drink, there are likely other things the devil convinces you to binge on. In the Western World, because of our great wealth, more is available making it easier to overconsume. Because of this, most of us struggle with a cousin of gluttony, known as intemperance. It's excessive indulgence or the lack of moderation or restraint. Every bad habit we have flows from this because it can be so hard for us to say "no."

Corporations make it even harder by trying to take advantage of this. They allow us to supersize meals at fast food restaurants, package snack foods in greater quantities, and enable us to watch any show at any time with the click of a button. Many of these companies employ scientists who create ways to make their products more addictive! They purposefully design our phones to light up and sound like slot machines, and lots of money has been spent on research to create systems or food flavors that reward the pleasure centers of our brains and keep us coming back for more. They understand how we work better than we do and profit off our ignorance. But this cannot become our excuse!

The devil loves how common it is in our culture for people to binge. One of the places that overindulgence seems to be culturally accepted is with technology. How many times have you binge scrolled through social media, played video games for hours on end, or streamed entire seasons of shows in one sitting? Any excess in these areas is not healthy, but some people get so sucked into the virtual worlds that they neglect their responsibilities and relationships. It becomes an escape from reality that feels easier than real life.

Without realizing it, many people use these escapes as coping mechanisms. Maybe they escape to gaming because they have a sense of control with the characters that they are missing in real life. Others may live vicariously through characters in the shows they watch. For some it's an avoidance mechanism to distract them from what they should be doing. (We'll cover this more in the sloth chapter.) Whether it's indulging in food and drink for comfort, or the coping mechanisms mentioned above, all these behaviors give us some sense of control. The problem is that it's fake.

It may seem that we have dominance over our behaviors, but the more gluttonous and intemperate we become, the more we are a slave to them. We might even internally hate what has become an addiction, but fear dealing with the reality of what life will be like without those crutches. Sometimes we must learn (or relearn) self-control behaviors from childhood. Tearing away from our coping mechanisms and compensatory behaviors is not easy, in fact it can be quite painful.

Lack of self-control is common in young children, so there is childishness to gluttony and intemperance. When self-control is absent it leads to selfishness, and the two are a downward spiral. In the movie based on Roald Dahl's classic, *Charlie and the Chocolate Factory*, there is a scene where these traits are on full display. One of the children, Augustus is so enamored with the chocolate river that he goes over and starts to lap up the sweet brown liquid. Willy Wonka tells him to stop because he is contaminating the chocolate, but Augustus keeps gorging himself. His mother seems largely unwilling or unable to rein in her son's behavior. It isn't until Augustus falls in that she becomes concerned because he can't swim. So many times, like this woman, we don't realize the danger until we are facing the imminent damage of a full-blown emergency.

There is nothing inherently evil with technology, food, or the other things we overconsume; it's the mindless consumption of them that is sinful. Gluttony and intemperance are parasites that slowly kill their hosts. Overindulgence in food destroys our physical health, and intemperance can destroy us and our relationships in many ways. Both are lethal to our relationship with God. When we fall into their traps, we are telling God we must turn to creation to find the fulfillment we cannot find in Him; this is a form of idolatry.

> WHEN SELF-CONTROL IS ABSENT IT LEADS TO SELFISHNESS, AND THE TWO ARE A DOWNWARD SPIRAL.

YOUR WEAPONS TO FIGHT GLUTTONY

On my birthday, about a month after I was first made a pastor, I was up in my suite smoking cigarettes. I had smoked for almost 20 years at that juncture; it was a coping mechanism, and I knew it. I had opened the windows to blow the smoke out because my secretary, whose office was downstairs, was deathly allergic to the fumes. I thought I was being altruistic by smoking upstairs with an open window, but then it hit me. I remember thinking, "Oh, for heaven's sakes! What are you, 10 years old and trying to hide your smoking from your parents?" I felt like such a child.

That was the last cigarette I smoked. I used the concern I had for my secretary as fuel and found a healthy way to deal with the behavior. Every time I had a craving hit, I would go out for a small walk. After quitting, I started to realize just how much time, energy, and money I squandered on smoking, and began to understand what it had been doing to my health.

Because this deadly sin, like all the others, is built on lies, the first weapon is again humility. If we let the devil deceive us into believing we need overindulgence to cope or find contentment, he will line up demonic slave masters for as far as the eye can see.

To begin to examine where the truth of humility is needed in your life, I suggest you gauge your reactions to the various parts of this chapter. What triggered you? Was it the food, gaming, TV, or electronic devices? Where did you get defensive and immediately think I was overreacting? Consider whether you used the token words of true addicts, "I can say 'no' when I want to." Did you resent reading any of these sentences? Lean into those feelings, they are probably a good sign that a little humility is required.

The next step is realizing that the object of your gluttony or intemperance needs to be eliminated as much as possible. In cases where you can't completely rid yourself of it, make meaningful steps to limit its use. To give an example, I'm as bad as anyone with my phone, so I've set up some guidelines for myself. One is that I don't take my phone to the table when I'm eating with someone. The more we can say "no" to things we tend to overindulge in, the better we become at mastering it instead of being its slave.

Taking steps like this is known as practicing the virtue of temperance, or self-control. As stated before, virtues are disciplines we build choice by choice. Each time we resist a sin, the more freed we are from it. It is built from a repetitive series of conscious right choices. It is not easy, but it is doable.

The next virtues to employ are generosity and justice. Justice is the cardinal virtue in which we attend to the needs of those around us. Gluttony and intemperance are rooted in self-centeredness and take up valuable time and what is due to others. For example, how many times have we been in the presence of loved ones and simply whipped out our phones and slid into our own little worlds? When people want to visit, they shouldn't need to hurdle the wall that the backside of our phone becomes.

By embracing generosity and justice, we train ourselves to put others first and to become selfless. In doing this, we train ourselves to love. This is the lesson the Church hopes to impart with every Lent through abstinence, fasting, and almsgiving. Lent isn't meant to be a 40-day reprieve from our slavery, it is supposed to be a permanent emancipation from bondage to our sins, where we learn to better love others.

As with all struggles in your life, and every battle against the devil, you need prayer. You cannot do any of this on your own. Instead of wasting time through intemperance, redirect that time to prayer. Make use of Eucharistic Adoration! Let it be a rock on your way to recovery. Jesus invites us to be healed of the crushing slavery of sin when he tells us,

"COME TO ME, ALL YOU WHO LABOR AND ARE BURDENED, AND I WILL GIVE YOU REST. TAKE MY YOKE UPON YOU AND LEARN FROM ME, FOR I AM MEEK AND HUMBLE OF HEART; AND YOU WILL FIND REST FOR YOURSELVES. FOR MY YOKE IS EASY, AND MY BURDEN LIGHT" (MATTHEW 11:28-30).

BATTLE PLAN TO CONQUER GLUTTONY

> *IF WE NO LONGER FULFILL THE DESIRES OF THE FLESH, THEN WITH THE LORD'S HELP THE EVILS WITHIN US WILL EASILY BE ELIMINATED.*
>
> St. Mark the Ascetic

1. **REFER** to The Core Battle Plan (Chapter 3).

2. **GAUGE** your reactions to the topics in this chapter and try to grow in humility regarding any triggers.

3. **CREATE** a plan to eliminate the objects of your gluttony and intemperance as much as possible. If you can't eliminate them, come up with some guidelines to reduce their hold on you.

4. **CONSIDER** how many times you've squandered resources due to acts of gluttony and intemperance. Be intentional to put acts of charity and your thanksgiving sacrifice higher on your priority list.

5. **EMBRACE** generosity and justice. Train yourself to put others first.

6 **PRACTICE** temperance (self-control). Build this choice by choice.

7 I cannot emphasize enough how the tools of abstinence, fasting, and almsgiving help break the tyranny of gluttony and intemperance. **IMPLEMENT** these practices as much as possible.

8 **FREQUENT** Eucharistic Adoration.

9 **LEAN** on prayer. Here's one you can use:

My Lord and My God,

At times, I have squandered Your great gifts through the childish sins of gluttony and intemperance.

Forgive me for seeking solace and comfort in the things of this world and not in You.

Help me master my appetites so that I may no longer be a slave of them.

Grant me perseverance in the fight and diligence in habit.

Amen.

CHAPTER 9:
WRATH

The BIG LIE

IT IS OKAY TO RETALIATE AGAINST THOSE YOU BELIEVE HAVE WRONGED YOU.

Though I am not a huge fan of *Star Trek,* I have always found Khan (one of the infamous villains) fascinating because of how well he encapsulates wrath. He is a genetically-modified superhuman who is overthrown in war, frozen, and sent off into space. After awakening he is so set on revenge that he manipulates a takeover of the main starship, Enterprise. This goes poorly for him when he's overthrown by Admiral Kirk and is again exiled. He is found *decades* later and is STILL hellbent on revenge. In his final defeat, the very last sentence he spews as life drains from his body, is a quote from the novel *Moby Dick.* "From hell's heart I stab at thee, for hate's sake, I spit my last breath at thee."

When we choose to succumb to wrath like Khan, we buy the devil's big lie that it's okay to launch a counterattack against someone who has wronged you. Wrath has a narcissistic quality about it. The wrathful person rarely sees their own sins but is quick to retaliate for any committed against them, whether they are real or only perceived. Khan is blind to his own evil and focused on his punishments, which he sees as injustices needing to be avenged. One of the reasons wrath is dangerous is because it is a sloppy marksman who always succeeds at inflicting collateral damage. Khan kills scores of people (ship-fulls actually) to get after Kirk because the ends justify the means. In this case, his quest for vengeance ends up killing all he loves and costing him his life.

Khan may be a fictional example, but there are plenty of real ones. Over the past few years, America has had a few highly politicized cases where a white police officer killed a black person in the line of duty. These were sparks that ignited a flame, fueled by feelings of a lack of justice and years of racism, suspicion, rhetoric, and poverty. Parts of the country exploded with riots, looting, and protests. Some demonstrations were peaceful and demanding justice, others were violently seeking vengeance.

We have a tendency in our culture to use the words 'vengeance' and 'justice' interchangeably, but the two are quite different. For many of the rioters, the only acceptable conclusion was that the officers be found guilty and have the full extent of the law thrown at them. They didn't care about the facts of the cases; they just wanted a result that would avenge perceived wrongs against their community.

Fair-minded people wanted justice. Justice is the principle that people receive what they deserve based on the choices they make. It does not always mean condemnation. Every day, men and women in this country are acquitted or found "not guilty" of the charges against them – that too is justice. Vengeance, on the other hand, sees condemnation and punishment as the only outcome.

Another example that demonstrates the difference between justice and vengeance began on April 19th, 1993. The FBI launched an ill-fated attack on a cult known as the Branch Davidians in Waco, Texas. The government believed the clan had illegal weapons and law enforcement entered with canisters of tear gas. Within minutes, the entire compound went up in flames killing 75 people, including their leader, David Koresh, and children. It was a great tragedy.

Three years later, on the same day in 1996, a band of domestic terrorists led by Timothy McVeigh, bombed the Alfred Murrah

Federal Building in Oklahoma City. It was an act of revenge for what happened in Waco, among other grievances against the government. The bombing left 168 dead and another 680 injured. Again, children were killed. McVeigh was put on trial, found guilty, and given the death penalty.

On the day of McVeigh's death, I was struck by President George Bush's remarks. "This morning, the United States of America carried out the severest sentence for the gravest of crimes. The victims of the Oklahoma City bombing have been given not vengeance, but justice. And one young man met the fate he chose for himself six years ago. For the survivors of the crime and for the families of the dead, the pain goes on. Final punishment of the guilty cannot alone bring peace to the innocent. It cannot recover the loss or balance the scales, and it is not meant to do so."

Herein lies the difference between justice and vengeance. There is a huge difference between what McVeigh did in Oklahoma City (vengeance) and what the government did in his execution (justice). McVeigh committed an act of wrath based on what he perceived to be true, the government found the truth and assigned consequences for McVeigh. We can argue the merits of capital punishment (for transparency's sake, I'm against it), but the execution did fall within the perimeters of the Church's teachings.

The examples of Khan and McVeigh are extreme examples where you are easily able to see the carnage and destruction of a person driven by vengeance. Although harder to spot, wrath can be every bit as devastating on a smaller scale.

Small-scale wrath can take many forms. The most obvious is when we take revenge by hurting another person, their loved ones, or their property. Many times, the attitude behind this is 'an eye for an eye and a tooth for a tooth.' People feel wronged and want to "get even." This is called *lex talionis*. It is found in the Old Testament in Exodus 21:23-25 and Deuteronomy 19:21. Some people interpret this as permission to take vengeance, but instead it puts a limit on it. The *lex talionis* could have been taken literally, but most of the time, rather than leaving everyone blind and toothless, money was given to the injured party.

A bunch of blind, toothless people would sure give you something to talk about though, which leads us to the more passive-aggressive form wrath can take — gossip. Gossip can come from a desire to fit in or out of boredom, but mostly it's generated by a desire to get even. There are numerous underlying reasons that trigger the inclination to hit back. Sometimes the target of gossip has wronged or rejected someone, other times they may be a subject of envy. Regardless of the reason, gossip is a cowardly creature.

Although active vengeance and passive aggressive gossip are the most overt forms of wrath, they are not the most common. The type of wrath that I've encountered thousands of times in my priestly ministry is an internal one – holding on to grudges. As the old quote goes, "Holding a grudge is like drinking poison and expecting the other person to die." Much of the time the grudge is held because the person was deeply hurt, damaged, abused, or humiliated. Sometimes a grudge is a result of a perceived slight. Either way, the primary person hurt by a grudge is the one who holds it.

Wrath is especially deadly to the soul as it actively and willfully withholds forgiveness and mercy from another. We pray in the Our Father, "forgive us our trespasses as we forgive those who trespass against us." In other words, "Father, forgive me in the way I forgive others." The wrathful person incurs the wrath of God and His eternal judgment.

In 21st Century America we love to judge, not just actions but people too. But the love of judgment comes to a dead stop when we are the subject. Then we want the opposite as we exclaim, "You have no right to judge me!" Doesn't Jesus tell us not to judge? It is one of the more troublesome paradoxes of our society.

We even love to judge people we've never met! The media leads the way by attacking anyone who doesn't think like them. If the target fits their agenda, the media will act as the arresting office, prosecutor, jury, and executioner, all before half of the information is even out. They do it because society craves it. We follow in their footsteps and join in the rash judgment blood sport against someone who likely hasn't done anything to us personally.

I've heard it said before that the devil calls you by your sin and God calls you by your name. The devil tempts us to identify ourselves and others by our sins, driving us to pride or despair. He wants us to believe that forgiving is a form of weakness that leaves us open to getting hurt again. The devil has a contempt for humanity, and he wants us to join him. He either drives us to an arrogance that causes us to redefine our sins away, or to despair that convinces us we will never be able to escape our mistakes. Forgiveness is a foreign language to him, and he wants us to need a translator too.

I believe one of the obstacles we face when trying to be free of wrath is misunderstanding what 'forgive' means. Too often we think forgiveness means to condone behavior, rationalize evil, or turn a blind eye. Forgiveness means none of these things. When God forgives us, He does not condone our sins or pat us on the head and say, "That's okay, I understand." To forgive means 'to no longer hold against.' If I forgive a loan, that means I set the person free from owing me the amount. If I forgive the debt, I can't come back and demand payment. When I forgive a person of their sins, I do not hold on to what they have done. I release it, like I have released the debt in the previous example. When God forgives, this is what happens.

But wait, isn't God himself wrathful in the Old Testament? What about the destruction of Sodom and Gomorrah? What do we do with 'Vengeance is mine, says the Lord" (Romans 12:19 et al)? Most of the passages like the previous one are pleas from God to not take vengeance for ourselves, but count that He will render judgment of the unrepentant. It is God who affirms eternal judgment, not us. Condemnation of souls belongs to Him alone.

We can condemn actions though. We can truthfully say that certain sins left unrepented leave one in true danger of Hell, but Jesus repeatedly warns us to focus judgment on ourselves. When we seek forgiveness for our own sins, we may see the sins of others more clearly. God renders judgment when the unrepentant sin is so great it endangers the good. When a person will not accept God's mercy, which is what He truly wants to give to them, then they are left with His judgment.

YOUR WEAPONS TO FIGHT WRATH

As with the other sins, we must begin with the weapon of truth through humility. This weapon, rightly used, informs us of our own need for mercy and forgiveness. It keeps us from the deceit of pride and hopelessness of despair by showing us that forgiveness is possible. It also helps us in being very careful about inflicting wrath upon another person. If we are aware of our need for forgiveness and mercy, from the vantage points of God and those hurt by our sins, we might be far slower in taking vengeance. Furthermore, if we are truthful, we know that the mercy we ask of God reflects the mercy we ourselves require. Humility helps us in going from a person of wrath to a channel of God's peace. It leads us to realize we need patience and assistance in conquering sin, and it assists us in being patient with, and not condoning, others.

Sometimes it is difficult for us because there are people in our lives who have embraced sin and offer no apologies for it. There are people who will continue to try our patience, hurt us, and who are otherwise uncaring about the consequences their actions have on others. We know Jesus says, "You have heard that it was said, 'An eye for an eye and a tooth for a tooth.' But I say to you, offer no resistance to one who is evil. When someone strikes you on [your] right check, turn the other one to him as well" (Matthew 5:38-39); and "You have heard that it was said, 'You shall love your neighbor and hate your enemy.' But I say to you, love your enemies and pray for those who persecute you, that you may be children of your heavenly Father, for he makes his sun rise on the bad and the good, and causes rain to fall on the just and the unjust" (Matthew 5:43-45). To do this, you will need temperance (remember, that's self-control) and fortitude.

Fortitude is courage in pain or adversity. It helps you to stand your ground and do what is holy and right when dealing with those who continue to harm you. If you follow Matthew 5:38-39, you are not to strike back or run away. To turn the other cheek requires resisting returning an evil for evil and instead, doing what is right. This type of courage is necessary, especially when loving your enemies may come with a price.

The most important weapons you can employ are the theological virtues of hope and charity. Charity gives us the willingness to see others the same way God sees them - as still within the possibility of redemption so long as they live. In modeling mercy and forgiveness, we mirror the love of God with the hope that such love might make our enemies seek what we have in Christ. Such a witness has melted the hearts of others and led to conversions.

Our ability to refrain from wrath is perhaps one of the strongest ways we show ourselves to be true followers of Christ. In July of 2016, I was a pastor at St. Clement in Bowling Green, Missouri. While I was away running a camp I co-founded, I received a call from the sheriff telling me my church had been desecrated. We later learned that a lady who had been a Catholic shut-in at our parish, who we regularly helped, was practicing Wicca. She had grown angry with God and released it by smearing her own feces on just about every consecrated item in our Church. This included mixing human feces with the Blessed Sacrament in the tabernacle.

The easy and understandable reaction to this would have been to lash out, but my parish and I knew what we had to do. Mercy and forgiveness had to be our collective answer. It was initially a bitter pill to swallow. My initial reaction on social media was to beg for mercy and forgiveness for the lady. I didn't have to beg very hard. By the time I had gotten back, parishioners were talking about raising her bail money! Some struggled, but everyone rose to the occasion and her daughters were amazed at the parish's response. The joy we felt when the Mass of Exorcism and Reparation was completed, and we could use our Church again, was influenced by our response to what had happened. We were all grief stricken when the lady committed suicide.

Forgiveness is tough. Vengeance and wrath are easy, but Jesus never calls for us to take the unchallenging path. He calls us to the narrow, often windy, road. Love of our enemies is what sets us apart as followers of Christ.

BATTLE PLAN TO CONQUER WRATH

> **IMAGINE YOUR ANGER TO BE A KIND OF WILD BEAST, BECAUSE IT HAS FEROCIOUS TEETH AND CLAWS, AND IF YOU DON'T TAME IT, IT WILL DEVASTATE ALL THINGS EVEN CORRUPTING THE SOUL."**
>
> St. John Chrysostom

To battle wrath, incorporate the following:

1. REFER to The Core Battle Plan (Chapter 3).

2. MAKE regular use of Confession and complete a daily examination of conscience. It is not another person's sins for which you risk Hell, it is your own – put your focus there.

3. STOP gossiping.

4. Are there grudges you have been holding on to? Try to **FORGIVE** and let them go.

5. DON'T join in on the media's blood sport of judging others.

6. PRACTICE temperance and fortitude. They are muscles that need to be strengthened.

7. CULTIVATE the virtues of charity and hope. Try to see others as God sees them and mirror the love of God through mercy and forgiveness.

8. PAUSE and think before responding, especially in situations where you can feel anger rising.

9. PRAY this prayer:

My Lord and My God,

Forgive me for the times I have taken vengeance through word, action or thought.

Help me to release those I hold under the weight of a grudge.

Help me to be as merciful as I know I need You to be for me.

Help me to turn from all forms of wrath through Your grace, and in doing so, show myself to be Your child.

Amen

CHAPTER 10:
SLOTH

The BIG LIE

YOU WILL ALWAYS HAVE MORE TIME.

If you've spent most of your life in Missouri, it's hard to escape native hero Mark Twain. This is especially true if, like mine, your high school years were spent in his hometown of Hannibal. On more than a few occasions, I wandered through the historic district where Twain's childhood home is located. It is here that the legendary fence from his classic, *The Adventures of Tom Sawyer* stands. In the novel, Tom's Aunt Polly tells him to whitewash the fence as a punishment for skipping school. To avoid the work, Tom tricks the local boys into trading him trinkets for the 'privilege' of working on the fence. Then he trades those trinkets for raffle tickets earned by kids who had memorized Bible verses. Young Catholics, this is what sloth looks like. Tom doesn't do any work yet reaps the rewards owed to others.

Many times, we think of sloth as laziness. That's not quite true, it's deeper than that and often doesn't involve idleness or listlessness. Frequently it's characterized by avoiding doing something good and busying ourselves with other tasks, taking focus away from what we are called to be attentive to.

One form of sloth that can be especially dangerous is acedia because it robs us of the experience of God in prayer. Acedia comes from a

Greek word meaning "a lack of care." The Desert Fathers of the 4th Century, who were early Christian hermits, called acedia "the noonday devil." As you can imagine, the middle of the day in the desert was brutal, so the monks would use this time for prayer. It is during this time that they'd find themselves struggling with wandering minds and being tempted to use the time to do anything *but* pray. I think most of us can probably relate to that. There are times where I will sit down to pray a Rosary or the Divine Office and my mind will squirm like a 2-year-old needing to go to the bathroom (I told you guys I spent a lot of time with toddlers growing up, didn't I?) Can you relate?

If a wandering mind doesn't resonate with you, surely you can relate to a type of sloth known as procrastination. We know what we should be doing, but instead of completing it we find ways to distract or preoccupy ourselves. Procrastination isn't always premeditated, sometimes it's like a sneaky ninja that creeps up on you. While I was trying to write this paragraph, I ended up taking a 15-minute internet tour of places in Colorado and college football scores.

Procrastination is a thief of time. It is the arrogant belief that God owes us another opportunity to do what He is calling us to do right now. The devil lies to us, telling us we can do it later and deceiving us into believing we always have tomorrow to get our affairs in order. Sloth and acedia are equivalent to hoarding time for ourselves. The problem is that time cannot be successfully kept, we can only misappropriate our use of it.

When I was in junior high, I was responsible for the outside chores. It was my job to take care of our half-acre vegetable garden, mow the yard, and clip and weed the flower beds. I'm showing my age here, but back then weed eaters were not common and our mower was manual, meaning you had to push it across the lawn without the help of an engine. It was hard work! Missouri summers are hot and humid, so on days where I was wise (and didn't let sloth get the better of me), I would get up early and do my chores before it got too unpleasant outside. I then had my afternoons to go to the pool or hang out with friends. On days that sloth took over, I would putter around and then remember that Dad's car was going to be pulling in the driveway at 5:30. I had two choices: hurry up and do a substandard job in the miserable heat or hope Dad didn't notice the unkept yard or garden and try again tomorrow. Neither was a great option, and both put me in an undesirable position.

In the Gospel of Matthew, Christ tells The Parable of the Ten Virgins (Matthew 25:1-13). These women are waiting for the delayed groom to arrive and have all fallen asleep. When they are awoken as he approaches, five are unprepared. They have not brought extra oil and their lamps are running out. The five wise women who brought extra oil do not have enough to share, forcing the five foolish women to leave to buy more. When the bridegroom arrives, the prepared women enter the wedding feast with him while the others discover they have been locked out when they return. It is too late. The parable ends with an ominous warning: "Therefore, stay awake, for you know neither the day nor the hour."

This same type of warning is issued in many other parables. Jesus calls for a perpetual state of vigilance. This vigilance is shown by our ongoing call to conversion and holiness. Conversion is not a 'one and done' proposition where we proclaim our faith in Christ and move on with life. The *Catechism of the Catholic Church* tells us "*Conversion* to Christ, the new birth of Baptism, the gift of the Holy Spirit and the Body and Blood of Christ received as food have made us 'holy and without blemish,' just as the Church herself, the Bride of Christ is 'holy and without blemish.' Nevertheless, the new life received in Christian initiation has not abolished the frailty and weakness of human nature, nor the inclination to sin that tradition calls *concupiscence,* which remains in the baptized such that with the help of the grace of Christ they may prove themselves in the struggle of Christian life. This is the struggle of *conversion* directed toward holiness and eternal life to which the Lord never ceases to call us" (CCC 1426). The proclamation of the Gospel and baptism begin a process. From that point on, we battle with our desire to sin. The devil takes advantage of this desire, but by the grace of God and our own effort, we can conquer sin and grow in holiness.

The person with acedia will look at tasks the same way a slothful person might look at them: they acknowledge it is there but lack the desire to take it on at this moment. They are like the five foolish virgins; they will hedge their bets and get to it later presuming that God will always give them more time. After all, wouldn't a loving God give them all the chances they need? Yet, like sand dripping through the middle of an hourglass, time passes and does not return. Sooner or later, the last grain drops, and time is up. Opportunities to make changes have passed. At the hour of our death, the time to answer the call to continued conversion and holiness ends and never returns. We may try to comfort ourselves with the sloth's view of God – that He is so merciful and forgiving that He will accommodate our sloth and lack of conversion, allowing us into Heaven anyway. But what about those ominous warnings of being shut out for all eternity? Sloth steals time to do what one wants instead of what is needed, and it leads down the broad road of destruction.

YOUR WEAPONS TO FIGHT SLOTH

For many in this world, comfort is a luxury, but here in the United States comfort is the norm. We dress in cozy clothes and most of us live in homes with climate control. We expect things to be easy and effortless. We eat junk food and fast food instead of going through the bother of cooking and cleaning up afterward. We watch endless hours of TV or mindlessly scroll the internet instead of engaging in learning, creating, or exercising. Our desire for ease becomes an enemy because it transfers to spiritual life. It encourages us to create a comfortable God who demands very little, enables us, overlooks our sins, and otherwise leaves us be. Discomfort becomes the enemy, when in reality it is your greatest ally in spiritual warfare.

Leaving your comfort zone is necessary for any type of growth. I've given this example before, but it's worth repeating here. If you want to grow stronger physically, you must exercise and do weight training. The exercise challenges your muscles and tears them. It's not a comfortable process, but it is through healing that the muscle mass grows. Those that seek comfort in their physical bodies have muscles that shrink and go into atrophy. The person who seeks discomfort through fitness has a physical body that is stronger, more flexible, and better at negotiating the rigors of life.

Similarly, if a person wants to grow smarter, they must seek the discomfort that comes from study. By study, I do not mean merely academics. For example, in the trades, hands-on experience and careful watching are necessary to master a skill. In some trades that means the discomfort of physical exertion that builds calluses, in other ventures the calluses are mental. The person who goes through the uncomfortable aspects of studying, masters a skill and opens themselves up to greater knowledge and creativity. The slothful person misses out and becomes more dependent on those willing to get uncomfortable.

In our spiritual lives, the same principle applies. If we expect to grow in faith, we must be willing to make ourselves uncomfortable. Certainly fasting, abstinence, almsgiving, and other mortifications help us exit our comfort zones and grow on the physical and spiritual levels. Growing in humility and seeking the truth of who we are before God can be unsettling as we recognize our sins and our failures. Conversion, by nature, entails embracing a sense of discomfort as one leaves habits, unhealthy coping mechanisms, and favored sins behind. To effectively do battle with sloth and acedia, you must be willing to get uncomfortable to earn the freedom of operating without the shackles of your sin weighing you down.

The first weapon I would recommend in this battle is the gift of the Holy Spirit called fear of the Lord. Fear of the Lord is a profound respect for the lordship of God. It keeps us from subtly or overtly making ourselves our own gods. It is humility that develops this because the person who seeks truth comes to the recognition of who God is. This helps us to take His call to ongoing conversion seriously, and to not tempt Him by presuming we will always be given more time and more opportunities. Like humility, fear of the Lord keeps us from putting off what needs to be done in the present. It drives us, out of respect for God, to become what He calls us to be and to embrace the conversion necessary to get there.

The second weapon is that of temperance. Temperance, or self-control, leads us to combat sloth and acedia by encouraging us to make the positive choice to engage in our duties. Sloth and acedia actively put off change, so in temperance we learn discipline to say "no" to the temptations that surround us.

The third weapon is developing the virtue of justice. Justice is when we render to another person what they need or are owed. Sloth and acedia hoard our time and energy by stealing the resources owed to God and needed by others. It means taking the time to pray and worship and ensuring that your relaxation doesn't come at the cost of your relationship with God. It also means making sure your responsibilities to family, friends, and workplace are duly taken care of. It doesn't mean we cease resting or taking care of ourselves, it is about balancing these things.

To give an example I often use as a pastor, I am an introvert in an extravert's job. In my earlier years as a priest, oftentimes, I would let my life get out of balance. I would 'get to prayer' when and if I could 'fit it' into my schedule. I would use the excuse that I was giving so much time to pastoral duties. Sometimes that was true, but often it was poor time management. It was me hitting the snooze button multiple times because I had stayed up too late watching TV or fiddling on the computer. For years, I took this to Confession and spiritual direction.

One day, my spiritual director looked at me and said, "Bill, you will always make time for what you value." The ugly truth slapped me in the face - I valued being entertained more than I valued prayer...or God. I had let acedia take over. I began to force myself to go to bed earlier, to quit hitting snooze in the morning, and get up to spend time in prayer. It was hard; however, now on the rare occasion I oversleep, I find my day unsettled if I don't begin with prayer. That doesn't mean the devil and his temptations go away, it means I find it easier to shake them off, especially when I am at Mass or praying the Divine Office.

Under justice, developing a sense of stewardship is also important. Your time and your unique strengths are gifts given to you by God. You are responsible for what you do with them. Think of The Parable of the Talents in Matthew 25:14-30, which follows The Parable of the Ten Virgins. A master gives three servants different sums of talents. A single talent would have been a significant amount of money. To one he gives five, another two, and to the third servant he gives one. The first two understand what is given to them and invest it. The third, takes his one talent and buries it. When the master returns, the first two bring their talents forward having doubled what was given to them and are rewarded for their stewardship. The last servant comes up and returns the one talent. He has not lost it, but he has also not done anything with it. This incurs the wrath of the master who takes it away and gives the talent to the one who had succeeded at multiplying the ten.

Each of us has been given abilities, advantages, talents, and spiritual gifts. These are given by God with the expectation that we will use them in a way that brings back a profit. Our investment is measured in how we use our time, energy, resources, and freedom. We either choose to hoard for ourselves, or we choose to build up an eternal relationship with God and help those around us. Think about the master's reaction to the one who had squandered the single talent or the outcome of the rich man who ignored Lazarus (Luke 16:19-31). The rich man ends up in Hell.

That is the price of staying in sin – Hell. It does little good to learn how the devil tempts us to sin, how we fall to sin, what we must do to be healed, and how to fight the devil if we don't actually *change*. Your soul is the battleground, and how much of the battleground is ceded is up to you. Don't let sloth keep you from advancing.

BATTLE PLAN TO CONQUER SLOTH

> **THE FACT IS THAT ATTAINING OR REALIZING A HIGHER VALUE DEMANDS A GREATER EFFORT OF WILL. SO IN ORDER TO SPARE OURSELVES THE EFFORT, TO EXCUSE OUR FAILURE TO OBTAIN THIS VALUE, WE MINIMIZE ITS SIGNIFICANCE, DENY IT THE RESPECT WHICH IT DESERVES, EVEN SEE IT AS IN SOME WAY EVIL, EVEN THOUGH OBJECTIVITY REQUIRES US TO RECOGNIZE THAT IT IS GOOD. RESENTMENT POSSESSES AS YOU SEE THE DISTINCTIVE CHARACTERISTICS OF THE CARDINAL SIN CALLED SLOTH."**
>
> St. John Paul II

To battle sloth, incorporate the following:

1 **REFER** to The Core Battle Plan (Chapter 3).

2 **CULTIVATE** the fear of the Lord, temperance, and justice.

3 **UTILIZE** the tools of fasting, abstinence, and almsgiving to shake you out of your comfort zone. These disrupt procrastination and are not just for Lent. They should be peppered throughout the year as spiritual exercises to help combat sin.

4 **MAKE** use of the Sacraments, especially the Eucharist and Confession.

5 **TAKE** time to pray and come to a deeper knowledge of our Faith.

6 **LEARN** to detach from the things of this world.

7 **ASK** for the assistance of the Blessed Mother (especially in the Rosary) and the angels and saints.

8 **BE** a good steward of all God has given to you.

9 **PRAY** this prayer:

My Lord and My God,

I ask for Your mercy for times I procrastinated in doing my duties.

I ask for Your mercy for those times I neglected the good of those around me.

I ask for Your mercy for those times I hoarded my time.

I ask for Your mercy when my mind wanders in prayer and at Mass.

With Your grace, I beg for the desire to do what must be done and to stay focused in prayer.

Help me desire You and the good of my neighbor before any comfort or ease the world has to offer.

Amen

CHAPTER 11:
BEING A HEROIC WARRIOR

Be not afraid!

On 9/11 the image that gripped me most wasn't seeing people fleeing from the gravely damaged World Trade Center towers, but watching people run towards them. On that day many first responders lost their lives, the first being Fr. Mychal Judge, a NYFD chaplain. He was killed when a falling beam struck him as he administered last rites to a fallen firefighter inside one of the towers. The bravery of Fr. Judge and others like him will be forever etched into our country's soul.

This book is a call for you to be that kind of hero. The kind that faces battles head on and runs towards the towers instead of away. In conquering the devil's influence in your life, you become that kind of warrior for those around you, especially those who are (or will be) placed in your care. Through God's grace, you are called to conquer the devil.

Becoming this type of person takes practice and skill. What you have read in this book is about training your soul, mind, and body for the hand-to-hand combat that battling the devil demands. You must realize that how the devil attacks will be specific to you and tailored to your weaknesses. He is a bully like that. However, as St. James reminds us in his epistle, "Resist the devil, and he will flee from you" (James 4:7). St. Peter reminds us in his first epistle, "Be sober and vigilant. Your opponent the devil is prowling around like a roaring lion looking for [someone] to devour. Resist him, steadfast in faith, knowing that your fellow believers throughout the world undergo the same sufferings" (1 Peter 5:8-9). With God's help, the devil cannot conquer you without your consent.

Remember, it is extremely important that you surround yourself with like-minded individuals who keep you accountable and are there to help you when the fighting gets fierce. One of my favorite Scripture passages is Proverbs 27:17, "Iron is sharpened by iron; one person sharpens another." Having others around you who are fighting in the same battles brings you strength. You help hold each other up.

Many years ago, I co-founded a camp for high school men called

Camp Maccabee. The intent was to give young men a little boot camp and the ability to build up fraternal bonds, creating comrades who stand shoulder-to-shoulder. We teach them at the camp that human help is not enough. We all need God in this fight. You need the supernatural to fight the supernatural.

The various practices of prayer, worship, fasting, abstinence, and using the Sacraments are there to help you get the supernatural help you need. Christ and His Church are there to stand beside you in battle.

Finally, young Catholics, don't be discouraged that you are tempted, and that God allows it. Allows it? Yes! God allows you to be tempted for your own good, so you can grow in holiness. In Chapter 13 of *The Imitation of Christ,* it tells us that "temptations are often very profitable to a man, although they be troublesome and grievous, for in them a man is humbled, purified, and instructed."

Battles help us grow in strength. I often ask God to help me with patience. So, what does God do? I get opportunities to practice patience because just like with anything else, "practice makes perfect." The same is true for all the virtues discussed in this book. Each one is like a muscle you build or a weapon you master. It is temptation that gives you the chance to flex and hone your skills and grow in holiness.

The devil knows all he can do is tempt you. Sometimes he will hit hard. Be aware that the closer you come to God, the more the devil will try to distract you with temptation. Jesus reminds us in Luke 11:21, "When a strong man fully armed guards his palace, his possessions are safe." God makes you that strong, fully-armed man. Use His grace, flex your muscles, hone your skills in the fight, and never forget who wins this war. Together, with God, we are an unstoppable force against the devil in spiritual warfare.

> "TEMPTATIONS ARE OFTEN VERY PROFITABLE TO A MAN...FOR IN THEM A MAN IS HUMBLED, PURIFIED, AND INSTRUCTED."
>
> THE IMITATION OF CHRIST

APPENDIX
OF PRAYERS

THE HOLY ROSARY

How to Pray the Rosary

1. While holding the crucifix, make the **Sign of the Cross** and say the **Apostles' Creed**.

2. Move to the first bead and pray the **Our Father**.

3. On each of the next 3 beads pray a **Hail Mary**.

4. In the space after the 3 beads pray the **Glory Be**.

5. On the next larger bead announce the first mystery for the day and pray an **Our Father**.

6. Skip over the center medallion to the next smaller bead. On each of these 10 beads pray a **Hail Mary** while meditating on the first mystery.

7. In the space after the 10th small bead pray a **Glory Be** followed by the **Fatima Prayer**.

8. Repeat steps 5-7 for the next four sections of one larger bead followed by 10 smaller ones. Each of these sections is known as a "decade" and you should announce and meditate on the second, third, fourth, and fifth mysteries, respectively.

9. On the large center medallion say the **Hail, Holy Queen** followed by the **Closing Prayers** and the **Sign of the Cross**.

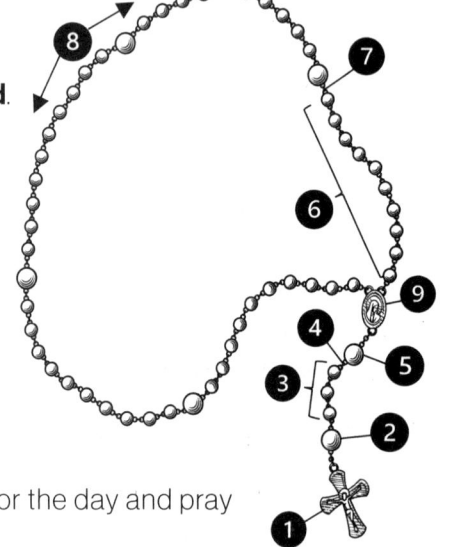

Mysteries of the Rosary

Joyful Mysteries
(Mondays & Saturdays)

1. The Annunciation
2. The Visitation
3. The Nativity
4. The Presentation
5. The Finding in the Temple

Sorrowful Mysteries
(Tuesdays & Fridays)

1. The Agony in the Garden
2. The Scourging at the Pillar
3. The Crowing with Thorns
4. The Carrying of the Cross
5. The Crucifixion

Glorious Mysteries
(Sundays & Wednesdays)

1. The Resurrection
2. The Ascension
3. The Descent of the Holy Spirit
4. The Assumption
5. The Coronation of Our Lady

Luminous Mysteries
(On Thursdays)

1. The Baptism of Christ in the Jordan
2. The Wedding at Cana
3. The Proclamation of the Kingdom of God
4. The Transfiguration
5. The Institution of the Eucharist

Notes

- During the season of Advent, the Joyful Mysteries are also prayed on Sundays.
- During the season of Lent, the Sorrowful Mysteries are also prayed on Sundays.

Prayers of the Rosary

Sign of the Cross

In the name of the Father, and of the Son, and of the Holy Spirit. Amen.

The Apostles' Creed

I believe in God, the Father Almighty, Creator of heaven and earth, and in Jesus Christ, His only Son, our Lord, who was conceived by the Holy Spirit, born of the Virgin Mary, suffered under Pontius Pilate, was crucified, died and was buried; He descended into hell; on the third day He rose again from the dead; He ascended into heaven, and is seated at the right hand of God the Father Almighty; from there He will come to judge the living and the dead. I believe in the Holy Spirit, the Holy Catholic Church, the communion of Saints, the forgiveness of sins, the resurrection of the body, and life everlasting. Amen.

Our Father

Our Father who art in heaven, hallowed by Thy name; Thy kingdom come; Thy will be done on earth as it is in heaven. Give us this day our daily bread; and forgive us our trespasses as we forgive those who trespass against us. And lead us not into temptation; but deliver us from evil. Amen.

Hail Mary

Hail, Mary, full of grace, the Lord is with thee. Blessed art thou among women, and blessed is the fruit of thy womb, Jesus. Holy Mary, Mother of God, pray for us sinners, now and at the hour of our death. Amen.

Glory Be

Glory be to the Father, and to the Son, and to the Holy Spirit, as it was in the beginning, is now, and ever shall be, world without end. Amen.

Fatima Prayer

O my Jesus, forgive us our sins, save us from the fires of hell. Lead all souls to heaven, especially those most in need of thy mercy. Amen.

Hail, Holy Queen

Hail, Holy Queen, Mother of Mercy, our life, our sweetness, and our hope. To thee do we cry, poor banished children of Eve; to thee do we send up our sighs, mourning and weeping in this valley of tears. Turn, then, most gracious advocate, thine eyes of mercy toward us, and after this, our exile, show unto us the blessed fruit of thy womb, Jesus.

V. O clement, O loving, O sweet Virgin Mary.

R. Pray for us, O Holy Mother of God, that we may be made worthy of the promises of Christ.

Closing Prayer

O God, whose only begotten Son, by His life, death, and resurrection has purchased for us the rewards of eternal life, grant we beseech Thee, that meditating upon these mysteries of the Most Holy Rosary of the Blessed Virgin Mary, we may imitate what they contain and obtain what they promise, through the same Christ our Lord. Amen.

THE DIVINE MERCY CHAPLET

How to pray the Divine Mercy Chaplet

1. On the crucifix, make the **Sign of the Cross**.
2. On the first bead say the optional **Opening Prayers**.
3. On the first smaller bead say the **Our Father**.
4. On the second smaller bead say the **Hail Mary**.
5. On the third smaller bead say the **Apostles' Creed**.
6. On the next larger bead say the **Eternal Father**.
7. Jump over the medallion; for each of the 10 smaller beads in the decade say the **For the Sake of His Sorrowful Passion** prayer.
8. Repeat steps 6 and 7 for the remaining four decades.
9. On the center medallion repeat the **Concluding Doxology** three times, and then say the optional **Closing Prayer**.

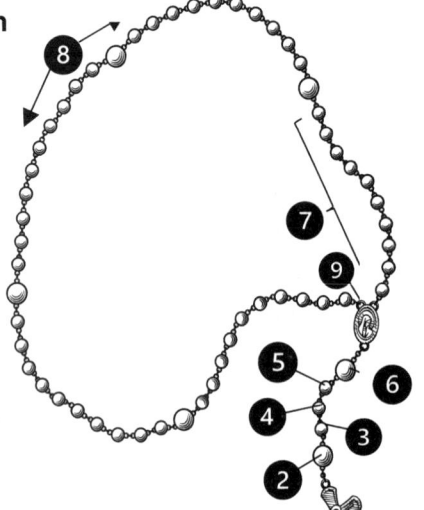

Prayers for the Divine Mercy Chaplet

Sign of the Cross

In the name of the Father, and of the Son, and of the Holy Spirit. Amen.

Opening Prayers

You expired, Jesus, but the source of life gushed forth for souls, and the ocean of mercy opened up for the whole world. O Fount of Life, unfathomable Divine Mercy, envelop the whole world and empty Yourself out upon us.

(Repeat the following prayer 3 times) O Blood and Water, which gushed forth from the Heart of Jesus as a fountain of Mercy for us, I trust in You!

Our Father

Our Father who art in heaven, hallowed by Thy name; Thy kingdom come; Thy will be done on earth as it is in heaven. Give us this day our daily bread; and forgive us our trespasses as we forgive those who trespass against us. And lead us not into temptation; but deliver us from evil. Amen.

Hail Mary

Hail, Mary, full of grace, the Lord is with thee. Blessed art thou among women, and blessed is the fruit of thy womb, Jesus. Holy Mary, Mother of God, pray for us sinners, now and at the hour of our death. Amen.

The Apostles' Creed

I believe in God, the Father Almighty, Creator of heaven and earth, and in Jesus Christ, His only Son, our Lord, who was conceived by the Holy Spirit, born of the Virgin

Mary, suffered under Pontius Pilate, was crucified, died and was buried; He descended into hell; on the third day He rose again from the dead; He ascended into heaven, and is seated at the right hand of God the Father Almighty; from there He will come to judge the living and the dead. I believe in the Holy Spirit, the Holy Catholic Church, the communion of Saints, the forgiveness of sins, the resurrection of the body, and life everlasting. Amen.

The Eternal Father

Eternal Father, I offer You the Body and Blood, Soul and Divinity of Your dearly beloved Son, Our Lord Jesus Christ, in atonement for our sins and those of the whole world. Amen.

For the Sake of His Sorrowful Passion

For the sake of His sorrowful Passion, have mercy on us and on the whole world.

Concluding Doxology

Holy God, Holy Mighty One, Holy Immortal One, have mercy on us and on the whole world.

Closing Prayer

Eternal God, in Whom mercy is endless, and the treasury of compassion inexhaustible, look kindly upon us, and increase Your mercy in us, that in difficult moments, we might not despair, nor become despondent, but with great confidence, submit ourselves to Your holy will, which is Love and Mercy Itself. Amen.

SPIRITUAL WARFARE PRAYERS

I HIGHLY recommend the book *Deliverance Prayers: For Use by the Laity*. It is full of powerful spiritual warfare prayers and explains the authority needed to use them. These are a few of my favorites but do yourself a favor and go buy the book!

Sealing Prayer of Protection

I ask Jesus to seal me in His most Precious Blood against any and all incursions of the evil one, in particular against any clinging, familial, familiar or retaliating spirits, in the Name of the Father and of the Son and of the Holy Spirit. Amen

Acts of Rejection: Another Form

I completely and utterly reject, with the full force of my will N. (insert any disorder one is experiencing or any evil one has committed). I do this in the Holy Names of Jesus and Mary and in the Name of the Father and of the Son and of the Holy Spirit. Amen (Thrice)

Prayer to Be Freed from Evil Habits

Give me, I beseech thee, O Holy Spirit, Giver of all good gifts, that powerful grace which converts the stony hearts of mortals into burning furnaces of love. By Thy grace, free my captive soul from the thraldom of every evil habit and concupiscence, to restore it to the holy liberty of the children of God. Give me to taste how sweet it is to serve the Lord and crucify the flesh with its vices and concupiscences. Enlarge my heart that I may ever cheerfully run the way of Thy commandments until I reach the goal of my aspirations, the joys and bliss of Thy habitation in heaven. Amen.

Prayers Against Temptation

Lord Jesus Christ, Who wast conducted as a criminal to the house of Annas, grant that I may never suffer myself to be led into sin by the temptations of the evil spirit or the evil suggestions of my fellow creatures, but that I may be securely guided by Thy divine Spirit in the perfect accomplishment of thy holy ordinances. Amen.

Come, O Holy Spirit, and destroy in me, by Thy sacred fire, every affection which cannot be referred to Thee or please Thee. Grant that I may be all Thine, that I may live and die ever true to Thee, my Love and my All. O Mary, my advocate and Mother, help me by thy prayers. Amen.

Prayer Against Every Evil

Almighty God, Father, Son, and Holy Spirit, Most Holy Trinity, Immaculate Virgin Mary, Angels, Archangels, and Saints of heaven, descend upon me. Please purify me, Lord, mold me, fill me with Thyself, and use me. Banish all the forces of evil from me, destroy them, vanquish them, so that I do Thy Holy Will. Banish from me all spells, witchcraft, black magic, malefice, ties, maledictions, and evil eye; diabolic infestations, oppressions, possessions; all that is evil and sinful; jealousy, perfidy, envy; physical, psychological, moral, spiritual, diabolical ailments. Cast into hell all demons working these evils, that they may never again touch me or any other creature in the entire world. I command and bid all the powers who molest me, by the power of God Almighty, in the Name of Jesus Christ our Savior, through the intercession of the Immaculate Virgin Mary, to leave me forever, and to be consigned into the everlasting hell.

Prayer to Overcome Evil Passions and to Become a Saint

Dear Jesus, in the Sacrament of the Altar, be forever thanked and praised. Love, worthy of all celestial and terrestrial love! Who, out of infinite love for me, ungrateful sinner, didst assume our human nature, didst shed Thy Most Precious Blood in the cruel scourging, and didst expire on a shameful cross for our external welfare! Now, illuminated with lively faith, with the outpouring of my whole soul and the fervor of my heart, I humbly beseech Thee, through the infinite merits of Thy painful sufferings, to give me strength and courage to destroy every evil passion which sways my heart, to bless Thee in my greatest afflictions to glorify Thee by the exact fulfillment of my duties, supremely to hate all sin, and thus to become a saint.

Purification Prayer

Jesus, pour Thy Precious Blood over me, my body, mind, soul, and spirit; my conscious and sub-conscious; my intellect and will; my feelings, thoughts, emotions and passions; my words and actions; my vocation, my relationships, family, friends, and possessions. Protect with Thy Precious Blood all other activities of my life. Lord I dedicate all of these things to Thee, and I acknowledge Thee as Lord and Master of all.

Mary, Immaculate Conception, pure and holy Virgin Mother of Our Lord Jesus Christ, draw each of us under Thy veil; guard me and shield me against all attacks and temptations that would violate the virtue of chastity.

Lord Jesus Christ, I beg Thee for the grace to remain guarded beneath the protective mantle of Mary, surrounded by the holy briar from which was taken the Holy Crown of Thorns, and saturated with Thy Precious Blood in the power of the Holy Spirit, with our Guardian Angels for the greater glory of the Father. Amen.

Prayer of Deliverance

Lord, have Mercy. God, Our Lord, King of Ages, All-powerful and Almighty, Thou Who hast made everything and who hast transformed everything simply by Thy Will. Thou Who in Babylon changed into dew the flames of the "seven-times hotter" furnace and protected and saved the three holy children. Thou are the doctor and the physician of our souls. Thou are the salvation of those who turn to Thee. We beseech Thee to make powerless, banish, and drive out every diabolic power, presence, and machination; every evil influence, malefice, or evil eye and all evil actions aimed against Your servant... where there is envy and malice, give us an abundance of goodness, endurance, victory, and charity. O Lord, Thou who lovest man, we beg Thee to reach out Thy powerful hands and Thy most high and mighty arms and come to our aid. Help us, who are made in your image; send the Angel of Peace over us, to protect us body and soul. May he keep at bay and vanquish every evil power, every poison or malice invoked against us by corrupt and envious people. Then, under the protection of Thy authority may we sing in gratitude, "The Lord is my salvation; whom should I fear? I will not fear evil because Thou art with me, my God, my strength, my powerful Lord, Lord of Peace, Father of all Ages."

Saint Michael Prayer

Saint Michael the Archangel, defend us in battle; be our defense against the wickedness and snares of the devil. May God rebuke him, we humbly pray. And do though, O prince of the heavenly host, by the power of God thrust into hell Satan and all evil spirits who prowl about the world seeking the ruin of souls. Amen.

Binding Prayer to Blind the Demons

Most gracious Virgin Mary, thou who wouldst crush the head of the serpent, protect us from the vengeance of the evil one. We offer our prayers, supplications, sufferings and good works to you so that you may purify them, sanctify them and present them to thy Son as a perfect offering. May this offering be given so that the demons that influence us (could influence us or name the person) do not know the source of the expulsion and blindness. Blind them so they know not our good works. Blind them so that they know not on whom to take vengeance. Blind them so that they may receive the just sentence for their works. Cover us with the Precious Blood of thy Son so that we may enjoy the protection which flows from His Passion and Death. We ask this through the same Christ Our Lord. Amen.

Prayer for Protection Against Curses, Harm and Accidents

Lord Jesus, I ask Thee to protect my family from sickness, from all harm and from accidents. If any of us has been subjected to any curses, hexes or spells, I beg Thee to declare these curses, hexes or spells null and void. If any evil spirits have been sent against us, I ask Christ to decommission you and I ask that you be sent to the foot of His Cross to be dealt with as He will. Then, Lord, I ask Thee to send Thy holy Angels to guard and protect all of us.

Guardian Angel Prayer

Angel of God, my guardian dear, to whom His love commits me here; ever this day (or night) be at my side, to light and guard, to rule and guide. Amen